The Heritage

Books by Ellen Bromfield Geld

STRANGERS IN THE VALLEY
THE JUNGLEY ONE
THE HERITAGE

THE HERITAGE

A Daughter's Memories
of Louis Bromfield *by*

ELLEN BROMFIELD GELD

Foreword by Lucy Dos Passos Coggin

OHIO UNIVERSITY PRESS, ATHENS

Ohio University Press, Athens, Ohio 45701
Copyright © 1962, 1999 by Ellen Bromfield Geld
Foreword © 1999 by Lucy Dos Passos Coggin
Printed in the United States of America

Ohio University Press books are printed on acid-free paper ⊗

03   02   01   00   99   5   4   3   2   1

First published in 1962 by Harper & Brothers, New York
First Ohio University Press edition 1999

Library of Congress Cataloging-in-Publication Data

Geld, Ellen Bromfield, 1932–
     The heritage : a daughter's memories of Louis Bromfield / Ellen Bromfield
Geld ; foreword by Lucy Dos Passos Coggin.
        p.   cm.
     Originally published: New York : Harper & Brothers, 1962. With new introd.
     ISBN 0-8214-1288-4 (paper : alk. paper)
     1. Bromfield, Louis, 1896–1956 — Family. 2. Novelists, American — 20th
century — Family relationships. 3. Novelists, American — 20th century —
Biography. 4. Agricultural innovations — Ohio — History. 5. Fathers and
daughters — Ohio. 6. Farmers — Ohio Biography. I. Title.
PS3503.R66Z75 1999
813'.52 — dc21
     [B]   99-32519

To my children,
Stephen, Robin, Michael,
Kenneth and Christina,
in the hope that my heritage
will be theirs as well

Contents

Illustrations

Illustrations

Foreword

For a young child in a literary household, life arrives in abundance and without much explanation. My father, John Dos Passos, continued to write and travel constantly during the last two decades of his life as I was growing up from 1950 to 1970. Sometime during his long life, my father had come to know Louis Bromfield. They may have met as ambulance drivers in France during the First World War. They were both from that same tumultuous generation of writers and adventurers who stirred up such creative turmoil during the early twentieth century. They both came to be caught up later on in the issues of the American farm and national agricultural reform.

Like Bromfield, my father lived overseas for substantial periods and traveled avidly to exotic destinations. Both men possessed great physical stamina and walked at a relentless pace over more territory than most people see in a lifetime. They both accumulated gifted, curious, and flamboyant friends who brought warmth and drama to their already-full lives. Although my father was never personally involved with agricultural reform on his family farm in Virginia, he had immersed himself in recording the developments of a good many farm movements. Roswell Garst of Iowa, who sold seed corn to Nikita Krushchev, became a lifelong friend. My father's travels involved a lot of first-hand observation. While in Brazil he got inside rubber boot factories and paper mills, embassies and whale slaughtering stations. If he heard that there was an experimental farm run by an American couple out in the coffee country of the State of São Paulo, it is not surprising that he looked up the daughter of Louis Bromfield. He probably saw it as following up on an old friendship.

There was little time spent on the past, however, with so many experimental crops to visit and stalls of massive Charolais bulls to admire on a neighboring ranch. The fascination of the next new story would rush in to overwhelm the lingering memories of the past.

One New Year's vacation my father heard that the Geld family with their five small children were all visiting the U.S. He rushed to invite them for the holiday. He spent so many quiet hours at his curving desk overlooking the Potomac River that he welcomed the happy commotion of a big family. He boasted that we had "a Geld on every sofa." He relished the creation of special meals and expeditions with all his spirit.

Like Bromfield, my father fought to keep up a frantic pace until almost the end of his life. He visited Easter Island with my mother, publishing a book about "The Island of Enigmas." They rented a tiny house in Head Tide, Maine during his last summer. My mother continued on at the farm in Virginia after my father died, but a great quiet enveloped the house.

For the last years of her life my mother was in a nursing home room. We brought her mounds of fresh flowers from her home garden. In early spring there were huge branches of camellias from fifteen-foot plants. Broad bundles of old-fashioned peonies followed, along with garish bearded iris trailing a faintly winey scent. What meant the most to her, though, were the gifts we brought at harvest time: the long ears of hard orange fieldcorn with every kernel perfectly developed. They would sit by the television with the boxes of tissues and cards from sympathetic church groups. Sometimes she would ask just to hold the ear of corn again to heft the weight and exclaim on the perfection of the rows of kernels. She would hold that corn and be connected to everything outside that was still young and productive and undeniably fertile. Her own nearby farm was right in her hands. She could relive that extraordinary season when the rains came just as the ears tasseled out and every strand of corn silk carried the message to fertilize a receptive kernel.

She loved corn, because it was such an American crop. She felt no remorse about corn's Native American origins, only pride in the largest, most modern ears. "American" to her meant the New World of North and South America. She had seen plenty of both. She could keep the nurses wide-eyed with tales of life on an island in the mouth of the Amazon "during the rainy season." They asked one another, "Did the lady with thick white hair in room 44 really once ride a water buffalo and eat South American crocodile tails?"

On special days the mail would bring a fat airmail envelope printed in green ink with the return address of Ellen Bromfield Geld, FAZENDA PAU D'ALHO, TIETE, SP BRASIL. For years she had corresponded with my parents. I was with them in 1964 when we drove up the sloping entrance road between glossy coffee trees studded with ripening red berries. The ample Geld farmhouse overlooked all the surrounding land and generously embraced visitors with a warm noisy universe of children, dogs, memorable farm food, and inexhaustible conversation. New crops, soil problems in the rainforest, gifted local musicians, hopeless political demagogues, the latest jokes about Brazil's ruinous future; there was time and energy for any topic.

Four years later I returned again during their winter season (summer in North America). We drove through murderous traffic from the turbulent cauldron of the mega-city of São Paulo. We arrived at night, but you could feel the same dips and swellings in the farm road. The farm crops and livestock continued to change endlessly to adjust to upheavals in the markets and gyrating economic conditions, but every square foot of topsoil was being carefully guarded and improved season by season.

For the next thirty years news of the Geld fazenda arrived by letter. After 1970, the year my father died, letters were addressed to my mother. The symbols on the envelopes reflected the agricultural stars of the decade, rounded Duroc hogs or Santa Gertrudis cattle with the stamps of Brazil recording the vast changes in currency values. Letters traveling in reply back from the United States told the story of our own family farm and the droughts and flooded basements of almost three decades. The loblolly pine seedlings of the years of the first letters were already slender forty-foot trees by the time my mother needed my help in sending news to Brazil of our growing population of bald eagles. She died knowing that her only granddaughter planned to visit the Gelds on a trip to Brazil to learn Portuguese.

First-hand reports of the Fazenda Pao D'Alho were exhilarating. Native plants were being reintroduced to the streambeds. The protected valleys were providing habitat for the noisy, long-legged sirieime birds. Their communal gatherings could wake a foreign visitor even before dawn. By afternoon the roving group would progress to the shade of the pecan orchard, all the while ridding the farm of any poisonous snakes in their way. They walked under the pecans on a carpet of a miraculous new pasture grass. The underground stems of the grass could bind up eroding soil as they spread and could withstand both heat and drought with impunity. The pecan trees had long since replaced the coffee trees of earlier visits.

Several generations of Gelds converged on the farm for an unrestrained reunion. A visitor could be swept up in such a swirl of loud and forceful characters. The grandchildren and great-grandchildren of Louis Bromfield celebrated, debated issues, and sang arias to the dubious cows out in the pasture at twilight at the end of a long rutted path.

After her visit to the Fazenda, my daughter began writing her own letters to Ellen Geld. Not yet twenty-one, there was so much to learn from a mother of five who could teach all of her children at home, write books in English while living in a world of Portuguese, and live every day with intensity. A young visitor could be wakened by the sirieme birds in time to be introduced to the milking of cows before returning to breakfast with fresh yogurt at a table where human stories, cattle, and pasture grass all mingled in the conversations of a literary farmhouse.

By the time I read *The Heritage,* the Geld family and my own had shared thirty years and two continents of experiences. There was a special excitement in reading about the early Bromfield ménage in Southern France. I could sense how the ancient European land-scape, formed by millennia of human habitation, gradually crept into the visiting Americans and fused with their own feelings for living on the land. The French farming tradition made possible the metamorphosis of the local soil and sun into incomparable natural products. Memorable wines and cheeses accompanied the sponta-neous mushrooms of the forest. The French taught their gift for transforming the entire natural world into an inviting menu, but one that could survive for each succeeding generation to savor. The local agricultural tradition demanded careful conservation so that the soil of France would always remain.

As Europe prepared to go to war over some of that same land, the Bromfields and so many other Americans came home from their gay European lives to face the reality of their own country. Louis Bromfield created a whole new future as he began the transforma-tion of the Ohio landscape of Malabar Farm. His beliefs in the power to heal and improve the land attracted widespread attention. Part of the family's way of life began to include teaching this new way of farming. Bromfield's books changed from the realm of fic-tion to the world of agricultural possibilities. He crusaded through his books, his public campaigns, and his own farm for ways to make a living from the land while living a full life as well. Bromfield was able to change the future for much of his acreage, but no farm is ever completed. The best it can achieve is to endure. Malabar Farm will now be preserved as part of our national heritage for the public to visit. Louis Bromfield left far more than his farm and agricultural beliefs as a legacy. His books remain as a gateway to his exceptional life. The Bromfield children inherited the freedom to invent their own lives.

Ellen Bromfield Geld with her husband Carson Geld created the singular world of the Fazenda Pau D'Alho in the state of São Paulo in the undeniably exotic country of Brazil. *Pau D'Alho* (The Garlic

Tree) is the name of one of her novels. The book evokes the feeling of a Brazilian farm life so fully that the reader, on finishing, is overcome with the sad nostalgia called *saudades* for a place that never quite existed.

The Heritage is an introduction to a treasury of writings by one of the United States' few literary families. Louis Bromfield and Ellen Bromfield Geld have shared their heritage with all of us through their books. As most of our lives recede farther and farther from the land we live on, these writings are a refuge. They explore how "the material and the spiritual ought to be united in the lives and works of men and move together in harmony" (*The Heritage,* p. 192).

LUCY DOS PASSOS COGGIN

The Heritage

1

Presbytère de St. Etienne

When we were children and just beginning to feast our senses upon the delights of being alive, we lived in an old Presbytère in the ancient village of Senlis, France.

The walls of the Presbytère, sunk into crookedness, had been seamed together again in their misshapen state with heavy bonds of ivy and soft, pale green and black patches of moss. It was aged and kind and tolerant, with the happy tolerance of a house which is decrepit yet indestructible. Within its white-walled sunlit rooms we could live expansively and messily without ever a thought about marring its beauty—for its beauty was far too old and solid a substance to be destroyed.

This was the house of my father, when he was young and headstrong and gay. And, indeed, there was something about that house and him which made them one and the same to me. Perhaps it was the quality of perpetual youth which clung to them both and which, in the case of the ancient Presbytère, made one feel that it would go on tasting and savoring of life until the moment when it dissolved at last into the dust from which it had arisen.

The Presbytère had once been the dwelling place of simple and austere Capuchin monks and had later been occupied by various bourgeois families, who had thriftily turned its ancient cemetery into a vegetable garden and led a life which must have been prosperous, placid and infinitely dull.

In view of such a past and remembering the way it was when we lived in it, I cannot help thinking that perhaps the Presbytère—so splendid and alive in the third century of its existence—had been waiting always for my father. For so great was their affinity for one another that with time the house became, like the dwelling place of a soul, a vast and simple reflection of my father's character.

His was a vital character, energetic, ambitious, insatiably curious about every human being, every manner of living. To be surrounded constantly by an assortment of human samples from as many walks of life as possible was, indeed, an obsession with him. And so it was that during the time we lived in it the rooms of the Presbytère and their numerous occupants were rather like a mass of atoms, which, without a magnetic central force to secure them, might have scattered in all directions and even changed in form. But as long as the force existed, it bound our strange, incongruous world together. The magnetic force was my father and, even if such a thing had been desired, not a room nor its inhabitant could truthfully have escaped his powerful influence.

Even in the nursery, which, in moments of arduous self-deception, Nanny considered to be a kind of bastion wherein young minds could be molded in an atmosphere of British honor, self-denial and restraint, there was always an air of waiting. It was as if everything, from the reading aloud of Milne and Dickens to napping while Nanny's knitting needles clacked in the afternoon stillness, was done with a hundred glances stolen toward the door, through which his tall, lean figure might burst at any moment, carrying with it a fresh wind of mischief and perversity.

More often than not, he would appear at suppertime to destroy with a nauseated glance our appetite for everything which comprised the boiled, measured, strained and fortified regime

2

which Nanny, at the daily risk of ultimate poisoning by the cook, valiantly ordered placed before us.

Shutting his eyes and screwing up his surprisingly elastic countenance in an expression of total disgust, he would groan horribly, "Good God, must everything always be predigested? Just imagine the spectacle when I introduce them to society and they're obliged to refuse le poulet au vin because it hasn't been passed through a sieve!"

While we laughed delightedly, he would put his head on one side and regard Nanny in the manner of one who had an unsolvable riddle. "Tell me, how did little Lady Couns resolve it? Did she ask for a plate of peeled grapes instead?"

This unkind reference to the little peeress whose upbringing Nanny had come to reminisce about more and more, since her descent into a hotbed of vulgar Americans, as the peak of her career, never failed to achieve its calculated effect. It was like lighting the harmless-looking little string which leads to a drill of dynamite.

"Peeled grapes, my . . ."

"Ah, Mademoiselle, attention—les enfants . . . !"

"Well, I'll say this for Lady Couns, whatever she did ask for she did it politely—something she had a good sight better chance of doing than anyone hereabouts."

Turning back to "hereabouts" Nanny would hover over our untouched plates like a little dark raven protecting her young, shooting furious glances from beneath bristling black brows and continuing to shrill at my father in a manner which other Nannies—even herself once long ago—would have considered entirely beyond their station.

"You are a perfect wretch, that's what you are. See what you've done? Oh, I do have such a time making them eat anything at all and now you've put an end to supper. Condemning them to a life of boils and rickets, that's all you're doing. One would think a man of your age would have a bit more sense."

He would make no answer, and regarding the havoc before him as if it were simply a demonstration of bad feminine hysteria not of his creation and, therefore, best ignored, he would step away to the long dormer windows which overlooked his lovely garden and watch for a moment as the tall poplars and purple lilacs faded slowly into the dimness of twilight. Then, wheeling about as if suddenly struck with some irrepressible inspiration, he would propose, with the conspiratorial air of a naughty child, that we wrap ourselves in sheets and run out into the garden to play ghosts. Or like an angler, experimentally dangling his bait, he would say, "Do you know? It's mid-autumn. The stags must be calling in the forests of Ermenonville. It would be a great shame to miss them."

Through the gold-rimmed glasses which balanced severely on her aristocratic, hawklike nose, Nanny would narrow her raven's eye dangerously and release a brand-new torrent of rebuke. But all the while her tongue clacked along its memoried path of resistance, her mind worked furiously to decide what clothes to put on us and whether to take a blanket and a Thermos of tea. Then at last, succumbing like an obedient servant who, after all, has no choice but to obey, she would forebodingly mutter, "Very well, I suppose there's nothing for it." And choosing at random from a memorized list of diseases, frightening and appropriate enough to suit the occasion, she would add her final thrust: "But don't blame me if they all come down with diphtheria." This said, she would bundle us into our clothes with Olympian rapidity, rush us downstairs and out into the car before there was a chance for the mood to pass and the master to change his mind.

For days after his appearance, the sunlit rooms of the nursery would be filled with a disquieting sense of adventure and naughtiness. And always, just before the dreadful pall of intended order and serenity was able to descend and smother us, the door would burst open again and all of us would be saved.

4

I often wonder if he would ever have visited us at all if Nanny, beneath her bristling uprightness and dignity, had not borne a poorly concealed longing to be off at dusk to the forests of Ermenonville to listen to the mating calls of the deer. But ever since the summer afternoon in 1929, when, squinting doubtfully at the pale infant form of my sister Hope, she had presented herself as Jeanne White, the new English governess, there had existed this crack in her armor. And it was there that, unknowingly, she had him. By this undercurrent of disloyalty to the rigid rules of her profession, she kept herself whirling steadfastly within his orbit. Then, whenever he was seized with a longing for childish innocence and naughtiness and the desire to dampen the abrasive lashings of a principled Scottish tongue, he had only to come and find us in the nursery, where we were—eternally—waiting.

There were other moments when he sought mischief of a more concentrated nature with no pretense at righteousness and not the slightest degree of innocence about it. Then, with a sheaf of papers in his hand and a good joke in his head, he would stride purposefully in the direction of another room where George Hawkins dwelt amidst deep, luxurious chairs done in authentic MacIntosh tartan, magnificent lamps dug up at a magnificent price from the graves of the Ming Dynasty, paintings by Sir Francis Rose interspersed with framed *New Yorker* cartoons and signed photos of all the best-known Hollywood and vaudevillian stars.

It was not unlikely (for anything could happen in such an atmosphere) that my father, upon flinging open the door unannounced, would come upon the rotund figure of his manager seated cross-legged on a tiger-skin rug beneath the ruthless glare of a sun lamp, like an elegantly mustached Buddha, clothed in nothing but bathing trunks and a tall silk top hat.

Holding forth his scribbled handful of papers, he would begin briskly enough, "Here's the next twenty pages of *Annie Spragg*. I'd like them typed before we go in to Par—" Suddenly,

5

the pages would drop, deprived of their crisp authority, from a hand gone limp with astonishment. "Good Christ, what are you doing in *that* getup?"

"I just got back from tea with the Marquise de Falconnier," would come the careless reply, coated, as it were, with the somehow undefiable armor of New Yorkese.

"The Marquise! In bathing trunks and a top hat? Have you lost your mind?"

"Lost my mind? Do I look like I've lost my mind? How d'ya like that? I go to fetch your brats from the château after tea and I'm asked if I've lost my mind. That's gratitude for you. Mind if I ask what's wrong with wearing a top hat to tea? I always thought it was an old Etonian custom."

Slowly, my father's humorous blue eyes would fill with a look of proper admiration. "You've got one hell of a nerve! But she let you in, all the same?"

The florid mustaches in the dark, sunburnt face that, deprived of the silk hat, could have belonged to an Italian greengrocer, curved upward in a grin, "You should have seen the performance *I* saw through the hedge!"

Urged on by the expectant light in the Boss's eye, George would transform himself miraculously into La Marquise de Falconnier, haute noblesse of the surrounding Oise. His short, bull's neck would seem to lengthen into a mass of thin, distended, nervous vocal cords, his calm, treacherous dark eyes to pop suddenly with a glandular exertion as, peering over an imaginary box hedge, he shrieked in a fit of horrified feminine agitation, "Qu'est-ce que c'est, Henri? Une bête de cirque? Un fugitif d'un hôpital de fous? Ferme la porte, vite, vite, dépêche-toi!"

Now his neck shrank back again to the wattled, healthless stock of a harassed footman who, trembling with gelatinous impotence at his mistress' high, peacock-like pealings, replied, "Mais, Madame la Marquise, je ne peu pas. Il n'est pas possible,

6

Madame. C'est le Hookans de Bromfield, nom de Dieu!"

"So she invited me up to the terrace in the midst of all those little monsters, dripping with éclairs, croissants and petits fours." Triumphant, wicked pleasure making those dark, luminous eyes his own again, George would spread his plump, competent hands and shrug. "What else could she do with 'le Hookans de Bromfield'?"

At this, my father would disintegrate into such an uproar of laughter that it could be heard as far away as the Convent du Sacré Coeur, on the most distant side of the village. And there the nuns, behind their stiff white habits, would nod to one another knowingly and smile and murmur, "Oui, mes soeurs, ce sont les fous Americains."

For want of a better one, "Manager" was the title bestowed upon George when he first arrived from the world of Broadway and Hollywood to become a part of the Bromfield household. In the strict sense of the word, nothing would have described him less suitably. But in George's case the title was soon altered to suit the man. It expanded, so to speak, and took on vast new implications, not the least of which was his ability to be mysterious. Wherever he went, he carried intrigue with him like a ball of twine, which, absentmindedly, he allowed to dangle from his pocket, unravel itself about everyone and everything as he wandered from person to person and place to place.

Certainly his coming into the Bromfield fold was a move enveloped in the kind of unearthly mystery that would touch all his actions in all the years we were to know him. It happened in the fall of 1929 when my father was in New York again, making ready to embark on a new career for the tempting sum of $2,500 a week as a writer for Samuel Goldwyn. Holed up in his room at the Hotel Algonquin, cursing noisily at the clutter of work around him and staring with gloomy longing at the crisp New York autumn day beyond his window, his thoughts were suddenly interrupted by a knock at the door. Opening it with some impatience, he found himself looking down at a swarthy, mustached figure, nattily dressed in a plaid sports coat, silk scarf and golfer's hat, a portable typewriter dangling from his right hand.

"I hear you're up to your ass in paper work," came the forthright greeting.

"Jesus Christ." My father gave an abject groan.

"Not quite." The little man's hat seemed to rise up on horns as he grinned. "But I think I can take care of this mess. My name's Hawkins. Goldwyn sent me."

With the roar of a liberated lion, my father ushered Hawkins into the room, at the same time stepping out and closing the door behind him. He didn't ponder, it seemed, the wisdom of leaving a total stranger alone in a hotel room with two thirds of his worldly possessions. Help had arrived. The autumn air and New York beckoned.

No one but a bellboy with milk and bread and butter spread with bits of garlic was permitted to enter the room for the next two days, at the end of which George emerged into the light with a brisk "That's that. Now let's go and celebrate."

Over drinks at Jack and Charlie's "21," my father tried to express his gratitude. "I really can't thank you enough."

"No need to," Hawkins replied in his already customarily noncommittal manner. "If you like, I'll stay on."

"There's no doubt about my needing help." My father regarded his new friend unhappily. "But I'm afraid the arrangement would be altogether too dubious financially. You know how it is with us writers—up one day, down the next. No, it's out of the question."

"Like hell it's out of the question." For the first time the spark that would kindle the entire Bromfield-Hawkins relationship, sometimes to the point of armed conflict with whiskey bottles, came into George's dark, melancholy eyes. "I may not look it, but I'm perfectly capable of sustaining myself in a state of pauperism. Money's no object. There's only one thing I will not tolerate and that's taking orders. I like to do my work when and where I goddamn please. That's my offer. You can take it or leave it."

At that moment, the possibility of George's making a top-notch secretary seemed highly unlikely and the years would certainly provide additional doubt in the matter. But so would time prove that practical qualifications bore as much weight as a grain of dust when Bromfield saw before him the makings of a great character. When my father boarded the train with his family headed for California, George and Nanny, already bickering noisily over the twenty-two bags necessary to accommodate a two-year-old child, brought up the rear of the procession.

Their sojourn in California was brief, gay and unproductive. After a year of not having enough to do, my father paid $10,000 to break off the contract with Goldwyn and the family returned to France.

That was in 1930. I was not born until 1932, and from the time I was able to distinguish one odd face from another, I naturally accepted my godfather, George Hawkins, as one more delightful and indispensable member of the Presbytère.

At the opposite end of the house, as far removed from the general circulation of daily uproar as possible, was my mother's room. And there was something about it which gave one, upon entering, the sensation of having come unexpectedly into a place of sunlight and shelter out of a constant enervating wind. Indeed, everything, from the little collection of Indian ivories on the mantel to the filmy curtains which so kindly let in the sun to the thin china cup in which my mother took her morning egg, bore the sense of delicacy and frail pacifism of the one who dwelt within.

It seems strange that anyone who so cherished peace and tranquillity should have come to dwell in a household where so little, if any, of either existed. But my mother had come, no

9

doubt, to answer to still another deep need of my father's, for rest and amiability and an occasional lack of defiance. And because of this, the role assigned to her was perhaps the most unpeaceful of all.

It was she who had, once a week, to announce to the cook, with a nonchalance that could hardly have been sincere in even the most insensitive person, that there would possibly be a hundred or so for lunch on Sunday. This alone was an awesome assignment—perhaps more awesome than the preparation of the lunch itself, which could be made more bearable by a series of French curses and martyred sighs. But there was as well for my mother the added knowledge that the "hundred or so" were bound to be a gathering of the most incompatible individuals (people who, on weekdays, dodged down narrow Paris alleys to avoid one another) ever to be brought together under a single roof.

Then, too, there was the continuous game of sidestepping, with pacific dexterity, George's intriguous twine; the need to rationalize my father's numerous explosions of literary moodiness; and, as if in penance for the otherwise often frivolous gaiety of her life, it seemed she was obliged to attend each Monday a long gloomy conference with Nanny over the depravity and deterioration of everything that was the Bromfield household.

Even now how clearly I can see our governess, a Scottish foretaste of hell's fire and brimstone, her feet planted squarely in the middle of the carpet of prettily woven flowers, insisting that "Madame really ought to take a stand" about the liquor bills; the interruption of the children's lessons by their father to go mushroom hunting; the latest chaos George had created by spreading false rumors in the kitchen.

My mother would hear all with a patient, defeated expression as though life presented in such a manner was far beyond her capacity to bear. Then, holding her cup with a hand so transparently thin that it seemed barely able to support such a weight, she would gaze wistfully over its rim at her antagonist. "Oh, Nanny, Nanny, can't we have some peace? Won't the mushroom season be over soon at any rate?"

Considering with suspicion the possible approaching doomsday of the mushroom season, Nanny would relent ever so slightly, shifting her weight to one foot and resting the back of her hand in a semi-fishwifely manner on the opposite hip. "Well, I don't mind telling you that doesn't help the liquor bills. All that shameless guzzling of Mr. B's whiskey, I think it's downright disgusting. And believe me, Cook's in a perfect tizzy. I wouldn't be a bit surprised if she didn't simply up and walk off without by your leave."

In spite of her physical languidness, caused in part by a chronic weakness of the heart and in part by an already vanquished desire to defend herself in the world, my mother's laugh was a big, boisterous Irish noise, at once reassuring and infectious. Her eyes, a moment ago mournful and persecuted, would fill now with humorous interest. "Cook's in a tizzy? What do you mean by that? Now, Nanny dear, I do wish you'd begin for once at the beginning. Tell me, what's George been up to now?"

Deflected at last, and somehow overcome by the peace she had determinedly come to wreck, Nanny would perch, still as uncomfortably as possible, on the end of my mother's pink chaise longue and sink into the time-wasting, frivolous oblivion of a good gossip.

By thus refusing consistently to "take a stand" about anything, my mother became, in a way, a screen between my father and the turbulent world he had created about him. I didn't understand my sensations then, being small and unused to tranquillity as I was, but whenever I came to play in that calm, sunlit spot which was my mother's room, I would find myself inevitably filled with a longing to remain.

Just beyond it, through a door which opened into a long,

narrow room, done in dark greens like a somber forest cave, my father sat, unaware of us all, writing down the things he thought, as he watched the swallows which nested under the eaves of the Presbytère sail out over the ancient roofs and Gothic steeples of Senlis.

There are some houses in which only those rooms which are the private habitat of one person or another have a certain personality of their own. The rest, though they may be variously colored and decorated, have a way of seeming monotonously similar, as if no matter what their owners do to make them different the dull, unvarying routine of the lives they lead within causes them to be inescapably alike.

But in the Presbytère de St. Etienne, even those rooms which belonged to no one but were used by all at different times were possessed each by such a singular manner and mood that one could change one's own attitude toward the day simply by going from one of them to another. For instance, if one wished to feel decorous, pompous and damnably false and ill at ease, one had only to pass from the flagstone terrace and cool, green garden, through tall French doors, into a large high-ceilinged room which bore the grandly forbidding title of "The Salon."

My father would have denied it with a spine-shuddering cry of outrage (for indeed such an idea seemed outrageous to him), but all the same I believe that The Salon grew out of a latent human instinct to possess and impress. It was a kind of mutation of the "front parlor" of American middle-class homes, full of polished furniture and hideous antiques—"the good furniture"—to be used only on occasions of death, birth and marriage. Yet, unlike the front parlor, The Salon was filled with really beautiful things: a wonderful selection of divans, chairs and tables of walnut and pearwood ornamented by handsome vases and china lamps, all in the splendid style of the reign of Louis XV. It was used only for the entertainment of persons whom my father decided, somewhat arbitrarily, bore a genuine knowledge and appreciation of perfection and beauty.

Perhaps these people should have sensed some privilege at having been chosen for The Salon, but there was a terrible something about the room, like a cold, unfamiliar segment of a person's nature which when it shows itself is astonishing and horrifying even to the person himself. Thus I am sure those "chosen ones," upon being ushered into The Salon's regal splendor, must have had the uncomfortable sensation of intruding, and at the same time being put on display, like so many more period pieces to be inspected, with a minute attention to detail, through a lorgnette.

It was, without doubt, the only unloved room in the house and would, in a question of limited space, have been the first to be eliminated. During the long periods of disuse, when countless unworthies were denied its handsome spectacle, it remained like an unattended museum, buried under a thick layer of dust which had to be hastily dispersed whenever the coming of someone fortunate enough to be considered "distinguished in taste" was announced.

One of the doors of The Salon was perpetually locked as if to avoid dangerous contact with what lay on the other side: an outlandish, mongrel combination in which walls covered with jungle scenes surrounded large, fat, comfortable overstuffed chairs covered with the same faded red denim material from which the trousers of the Brittany fishermen are made. The red of the chairs alone was a color warm and lively enough to make one feel immediately gay and at ease. But the sight of them cast adrift, like lost Brittany seafarers, in the midst of a maze of tall, shadowy acacia trees, flamboyant and giant philodendrons through which elephants lumbered, panthers crept and monkeys swung on jungle vines, was enough to put not only formality but all sense of inhibition aside.

Those incredible walls were the result of a trip taken to India in 1936 by my parents, George and our good friend Anne

13

Chamay, who lived in Senlis, not far from the Presbytère. Upon their return, as if seized with a passion to express the exotic color and vividness of India while it was still fresh in their minds and save some sample of it for when the memory had grown cold and detached with age, all four travelers had hastily set about covering the wall of the Red Room with jungle scenes.

So unlike were the personalities of the artists, each with a definite bent for the role of the prima donna, that one might have expected to find in those scenes, which covered the Red Room from floor to ceiling, nothing more than a conflicting hodge-podge of four amateur self-reflections. But the murals were strangely harmonious, flowing one into the next, so that even here it seemed the creation had been dominated and guided by the most powerful imagination of all.

It was in this room, which we called the Red Room, that the more favored guests remained after Sunday lunch to gossip, philosophize and perform for one another to the accompaniment of lively and beautiful music, the sound of which continued on far into the night.

Each Sunday, those guests gathered for lunch in what had once been the austere refectory of the Capuchin monks and which was now adorned with handsome gilt mirrors, crystal chandeliers, a long, hospitable cherry-wood table and a fine old eighteenth-century Valois buffet, which sagged a little with the combined weight of the lavish meals and its great age. Sometimes the guests were as many as a hundred, overflowing onto the terrace and into the shaded corners of the garden. The more of them there were, and the greater the variety, the better, for my father loved to mix people as one combines all sorts of uncongenial spices to produce a rare and marvelous chutney. So it was that a Sunday visitor was likely to find himself spending the afternoon on the terrace, telling jokes and discussing politics with Gertrude Stein, Leslie Howard and the Maharaja of Baroda.

The sound of their conversation, full of wit, sarcasm and noisy laughter, shattered the quiescent peace of a French village at Sunday afternoon's rest. And, from the nursery, we children watched with critical eyes, as if indeed all those talented and brilliant people had gathered to perform for our benefit alone. Sometimes we repaid them for entertaining us by tossing down water from a pitcher; an act which we always hoped might flatten the hairdo of Madame Robert de Rothschild or douse the startled spine of Alice B. Toklas. But, alas, our efforts were usually wasted on simply increasing the cool dampness of the Presbytère's tolerant and enduring ivy-covered walls. Only once did my sister Hope make a bull's eye, landing not only the water but the pitcher as well squarely upon the head of a guest whose name now escapes me, perhaps because (although, his skull streaming with blood, he assured us the blow was "nothing at all") we never heard of him again.

In spite of such entertaining diversions, we always watched with relief as the last Fiat and Rolls-Royce turned the corner of La Rue de Presbytère and sped off in the direction of Paris, whence they had come. For their departure meant for us the coveted prize of Sunday-night supper in the kitchen. There, on the vast wood stove which cast its cheery light across the white walls and red-tiled floor of that large and useful room, my father destroyed the purpose of our weekday's puréed fare by concocting quiche aux morelles, soupe à l'oignon, omelette aux fines herbes. And, when at last we had devoured this ruinous meal with what must have been an innate instinct for chewing, and topped it off with Nanny's special corruption of indigestible English toffee, we gathered in the Green Room for an evening of ballet.

We set the stage by draping everything with the loveliest frail silken saris from India, and when all was in readiness, my father would toss me, Sobahide, ceilingward, with all the force and passion of an enslaved lover. George inevitably played the part of the Sultan, turbaned now, rather than silk-hatted, in a head-

gear stolen from the cabin of an indignant Sikh aboard an
Indian tramp steamer upon safe arrival in the port of Bombay.

As I drifted downward, my toes pointed sharply to meet the
oncoming carpeted floor, he sat cross-legged on a heap of cushions,
sipping vodka and munching crackers spread with caviar, patiently awaiting his cue to stab me with a pâté knife and toss
me to the end I had so faithlessly earned.

I think more than any of the others we loved the Green Room,
with its odds and ends of furniture, its shelves of worn books,
in the midst of which the bust of Voltaire sat, observing all with
his perpetual look of amused cynicism. For it was here that, once
the great world of which my father had struggled so successfully
to become a part had finally taken its leave, we came together at
last as a family.

There was always an air of festivity about the occasion, as if
the discovery that one's own family also possessed the ability to
be congenial and entertaining was indeed a cause for celebration.

And so we celebrated through all the years in the Presbytère.
It was a vital life which all of us led, born out of one man's
intense desire to live and to know. No pleasure of living escaped
us then, from the knowledge of cold, starlit autumn nights in
the forests of Ermenonville, to the close, earthy enchantment of
mushrooms hunted by day among the young grasses of spring,
and eaten ravenously at night with wine by firelight in the
kitchen. Ever since those early days, certain unforgettable strains
of music have followed me all my life, so that upon hearing
them I am inclined to smile strangely and with fond recognition
upon ghosts dancing in a cluttered, sari-strewn room or laughing
and talking together in the cool of an evening on a flagstone
terrace overlooking a little river called the Nonnette.

The ghosts are almost faceless now, but the sensations upon
meeting them are all the clearer: the sensations of laughter and
warmth and eagerness and deep enjoyment. There must have
been anger and sadness as well, for we were brought up violent

and possessive of our emotions as savages. But of these I remember only occasional instances of comic rage of the kind which relieves, like a cloudburst after a long and hotly thunderous day.

I suppose this first impression could well be called "A Portrait of the Artist in His Most Optimistic Youth" by a daughter who was far too young to understand its intricacies. But I prefer to think that what I saw then were flashes of truth, uncluttered by the prejudices and lengthy ponderings of later years. Thus, I can further allow myself to believe that the memory of the Presbytère was the real portrait, and the rest which followed something dulled by the shadows which life casts over all of us, until, in the end, it is difficult to discern whether or not a man is what in the beginning he so valiantly set out to be.

 2

Of Roots and the World

My father was born in the small Midwestern town of Mansfield, Ohio, just at the turn of the century when the great industrial revolution had begun to sweep ponderously, but with deadly certainty, over the land, changing everything forever. Yet he never loved the town. It was the Ohio wild country, still lush and green and a little untamed, that he loved: the country into which his ancestors had walked from beyond the Alleghenies a century before to lay claim to what was then the new land.

The era in which my father was born had already caused a great many of those old and substantial farmers to leave the land —among them, his own family. But they were still country people at heart with still some memory of a time when one's land was richly sufficient unto itself and, if he pleased, a man could actually live independent of the entire world.

They were strong people who knew how to look after themselves in difficult as well as prosperous times. Individualism to them was not a matter of being untidy, rude and rebellious toward society, but of living with dignity according to their own beliefs and not those of the next man's. It was as simple as that: the kind of individualism which is only possessed by people who have long worked with both their hands and their brains and are not afraid of being alone. And even though my grandparents, Charlie and Nettie Bromfield, made their life in the

18

town, that powerful individualism clung to them still and often gave itself vent in strange and wonderful ways.

My grandfather made his living as an employee in a bank and, from time to time, as a politician. But the business of working simply to make money never really caught his imagination. And, although he loved the side of politics which dealt with roaming over the countryside meeting and talking to people, the side which had to do with chicanery and meanness evaded his interest altogether. Often he longed to escape, if only temporarily, a life which, because it didn't suit him, was constantly beset with failure and disappointment. And so, whenever he could "get away," he would head for the Ohio wild country with his son at his side.

It was a land of forested hills and countless fertile, hidden valleys, where a man and a boy could wander endlessly, always with the expectation of discovering just beyond the next ridge a new and enchanted world. Sometimes it was a cave, deep in the forest, formed when the great glacier passed that way, changing all the earth with its massive weight and leaving strange formations of beautiful yellow and pink sandstone in its wake. The caves offered up an eerie darkness, speckled with sunlight and strewn with arrowheads, which recalled, with a shuddering excitement, a time now lost and behind them. Sometimes it was a stream which cut through a fertile valley and into the wood to a place where the current was blocked by the fallen trunk of an aged tree. And sometimes it was an old house, weathered and haunted, set in the midst of a field choked with poison ivy and blackberry brambles, beneath whose thorny sweetness the earth told a tale of ruin, poverty and abandonment.

It was perhaps the last which held its greatest attraction for the wistfully dignified gentleman whom we shall always remember as Pa Bromfield. For he was the first of us to have been possessed with a mania which has continued on through his seed in the generations that followed: the uncontrollable desire to bring back to life from the sadness of abandonment old farms which had once known the great happiness of fertility. Perhaps it was really a desire to recall an old life which would have suited him well, in which every breath and movement was busy and creative and born of the very richness of the earth. Or perhaps, because of countless disappointments encountered in the world of men, he had become convinced that nothing was quite so worth saving as the earth itself. At any rate, that same irrepressible desire would come, in the end, to occupy all his son's energies as well, almost to the point of wearing him to death. And in still another generation, it would have my sister farming diligently and defiantly in the midst of a decadent Virginia countryside, where most of the land had been taken over by poor white trash or people who spent their lives riding to hounds; while I would be driven to one of the last frontiers of the world, where the old life would be recalled for a time, only to be destroyed by the same blind, greedy, speculative force which destroyed so much of the Ohio countryside at the time of my father's youth.

Pa's ventures in saving old farms always ended in failure because of an acute lack of funds to carry them out. But through them his children discovered the whole cycle of birth, life, death and rebirth which is the cycle of nature, as beautiful as it is indestructible. They knew what it was to love earth and to respect it above all else as the beginning and the end of everything. And so my grandfather's time and money and energy were far from wasted. He had a good time. That in itself was enough. But beyond that, he passed his mania on to his progeny, so that for them, no matter what happened, there would always be a certain basic sense to life—something to turn back to. In disappointing times, they would be able to stand off to one side and see themselves as part of a great, complex pattern and, in its very intricacy and enormity, find a strong and satisfying solace.

Pa was never ambitious in a worldly way, and yet most of his life was spent doing jobs he disliked in order to acquire for his family a place in a success-hungry materialistic world which, in his mild, polite manner, he despised. My grandmother, on the other hand, restless and energetic and intensely ambitious, was forever withheld by the customs of her era and her duties as a housewife from putting her tremendous zeal to its ultimate test. She would, no doubt, have made a far better politician than Pa, for she didn't mind telling a lie or performing a distasteful task if it served the proper purpose. But, because she could not barnstorm the country fighting for woman's suffrage or negotiate great financial coups, she released all her tremendous contriving energy upon her children.

Surrounded by the smug, self-satisfied atmosphere of the town in which she lived, she struggled valiantly to teach her children something of the world. She found ways to give them a basic knowledge of great music, even though her own conception of music never went beyond the mucky sentimentality of "Ah, Sweet Mystery of Life" and her favorite, "The Baggage Coach Ahead." She made them read classics which she herself had never opened, so that the knowledge they acquired might excite in them a curiosity which could never be satisfied within the bounds of the town and the lovely, compact hills and valleys they already knew so well.

And so it was that, through his parents' frustrated longings, my father as a boy lived haunted by two desires: that which Pa had instilled in him in their wanderings through the wild country, to settle on the land and take root; and that other desire, kindled by Ma with all the strength of her immense will, to know and conquer the world.

For a time it seemed that the powerful earth would succeed in securing him permanently with the bonds which had been created long ago, when first he had followed the course of a stream into the depth of a wood. Half drawn by a sense of duty, a longing to repay and replenish all the goodness he had known, he set about trying to restore the family farm, which, itself, had fallen into ruin since the family had been forced to desert it, one by one, for the town. But the daily routine of physical labor, once so satisfying, seemed now to stretch before him in an inescapable monotony in which knowledge was limited to what lay within the scope of his vision. And all the time, beyond the hills which bound his daily vision, there lay that strange, glamorous, sensual, vital world which he had glimpsed behind closed eyelids on nights when, after putting aside Dickens or Thackeray or Balzac, he had tried vainly to think of tomorrow's nearness, and to sleep.

Pa Bromfield's sense of values and ability to separate things of consequence from vanity and nonsense were a part of my father. But the old gentleman's patient acceptance of what life had to offer was not. Already at seventeen there was stirring in my father's blood a terrible sensation that life was infinitely short and that, if any of it was to be seen and known, it must be sought, plunged after and seized upon. There was no time to sit, as he was sitting, and wait. So, in the end, Ma's ceaseless connivances triumphed with a far greater success than even she had expected. Full of eagerness for a knowledge it seemed he could never find in the small world in which he had been born, he went first to spend a fitful year at Cornell, studying agriculture; and when this proved less inspiring than he had expected, he turned to Columbia University to study journalism.

This was to have been the starting point from which, once armed with scholarly achievements, he would go out and explore whatever there was to be explored. But somehow Columbia was no less disappointing than Cornell or the farm. Studying only seemed to increase his impatience, so that, sitting, listening to long, theoretical lectures, his eyes wandered to the windows and contemplated the immensity of the sky. The air in the room became stifling. The very artificiality of university life—sheltered, dedicated to thought and debate and occasional forced gaiety—

became somehow more oppressive than the life on the farm, where at least each day there occurred a new phenomenon, if only the sprouting of a mushroom. With time, it became more and more reasonless to him to discuss and interpret the writings of men who had lived and experienced the world, without first having lived in it and experienced it himself.

In the end, as for many, it was the First World War which provided his escape. In 1914, despite Ma's scenes and tirades and weeping protests, he joined an ambulance corps attached to the French Army and went off to France. Thus, like a young man from the dry plain who has all his life dreamed of tasting the stinging, turbulent waters of the sea, he plunged into a world of war.

It was a lucky thing that, in this way, he chose to wander before taking root. For had he decided to remain and farm, that ambitious, curious soul of his would have become dry and bitter, dwelling upon all he had missed. Unfed by the experience and a knowledge of the world, his roots would have withered in an earth whose infinite value he could never have come to understand. As it was, like a kindly, experienced older woman who knows how to live and wishes to impart her knowledge to someone young and eager for life whom she loves, France introduced him to a world which was at once earthy and flamboyant, tolerant and highly civilized. There was little in it of the stuffy self-righteousness and intolerance of the small Ohio town from which he had come. It was a world which placed a higher value upon wit, humor and learning than upon material success. Wealth or poverty, already long established and almost unalterable, were not of great importance. In France he discovered one lived as one liked and, as a whole, one's extraordinary thoughts were encouraged and debated rather than condemned as eccentric.

Later on he would write of it, "France, a country where I had never been a stranger, even on that first night when I stepped ashore at Brest at the age of eighteen and tasted my first French cheese and French wine in the smoky, smelly little bars and cafés of the waterfront." At the age of eighteen, he had escaped. And by the time the war had come to an end he had already lived a great deal. He was at home in the world, and from it he could see his own country with a new and keen perception.

It was not my father alone in whom Ma, with her powerful will, had instilled enormous curiosity. All three of her children had, at one time or another, broken away from the unimaginative world of Mansfield, Ohio. All of them had found their way to New York. But my father's sister, Marie, and his brother, Charles, were to discover that, in order to survive in a world of luster, it is necessary to bring along a considerable luster of one's own.

Marie, who was, according to all my father's descriptions, a spirited, beautiful and talented woman, came to New York as a concert pianist. But, held back by a husband who hadn't the vigor and charm to match her own, she lived a tragically dreary life until she died of double pneumonia in 1935.

Charles came to New York years later and, on the coattails of his elder brother's success, began a lively career as an intelligent and charming young playwright. But he too lacked vigor and ambition necessary to make a success. He never achieved recognition and finally gave up writing altogether.

Perhaps Charles and Marie would have been happier had they remained in the less vicious surroundings of the small town from which they came. For New York can prove bitter surroundings for those who don't achieve success. Of the three, only my father found, in the end, all that he sought in New York. For him, on his return from Paris in 1919, the surroundings came as near as possible, without turning dull, to perfection.

As a young man in search of opportunity, he came across some of the great city's most miserable facets as well as its brightest. One of his first jobs was to cover the mental wards of Bellevue

Hospital for the New York News Service. For a sensitive and healthy person who would rather have maintained the illusion that illness was nonexistent, the hopelessness of Bellevue must have been more oppressive than anything he had yet experienced —even more so than his two years at war, during which he remained almost constantly in the front lines, and for which France awarded him the Croix de Guerre.

But Bellevue was not the center of his life for long. In a manner that had been typical of him even as a boy, he was soon handling more jobs than seemed humanly possible. Between 1920 and 1924, he was night editor for the Associated Press, foreign editor for *Musical America,* assistant to Brock Pemberton, the theatrical producer, music critic for both *The Bookman* and *Time* magazine, and, finally, advertising manager for G. P. Putnam's Sons. It would have been difficult even for him to remember which jobs came when, or how many of them he held down at a time. His career became more complicated, busy and prosperous with every year in New York.

Everything seemed to turn in his favor. A handsome young man, tall and well built with a sensitive yet strong face, his candid blue eyes held neither the expression of bored sophistication of many of his contemporaries nor the innocence one might have expected in a young man from the edge of the western plains. There was in his gaze an easy, unsuspicious friendliness and humor as well as undisguised curiosity. For in all human beings he found the makings of a story, flattering or not. The more complicated the person, the more charming, the more apparent a touch of deviltry that for all good intentions could not be repressed, the more my father was apt to like him.

There were perhaps only two qualities he could never tolerate: and those were self-righteousness and a lack of humor. Wherever he encountered them, he became taciturn and rude. But even this caused, not only those who were more favored, but some of his victims as well to love him. For it proved in him still another hard-to-come-by quality. He was direct and sincere. He knew what he wanted. He knew what was worth while in life.

Surely this was the first thing that attracted Mary Appleton Wood, my mother, direct and sincere as she was herself. She had been sheltered all her life within the aloof confines of an old New England family, and the appearance of this gay, strong young man from the West must have been something like a fresh wind in a musty attic. She had always regarded the great world with longing from behind the boundaries of New England society and the New York Social Register. Because of this, I imagine that for her my father *was* the great world.

I am just as sure, as well, that, amidst the incredible jumble of theater people, socialites, Bowery bums, newsmen and writers who were my father's friends, this innocent young woman from a dowdily aristocratic background must have held a powerful fascination. Certainly my father found in the world from which she came enough enchantment to write, later on, the Pulitzer Prize–winning novel *Early Autumn*. But once she drew aside the curtain to this world, he found her in its midst, a tender woman with a sense of balance and humor that was at once soothing and profound.

Ma Bromfield, who had come by then to station herself in New York as the snarling protectress of her wandering progeny, disapproved of the match. She remained dogged in her conviction that the only New Englanders of any worth had left that barren, rocky land for the green hills of the Midwest long ago. But, of course, any needling on Ma's part only served to heighten my father's contrary desire. Mary Appleton Wood and Louis Bromfield were married in the fall of 1921, and my mother for the first time plunged headlong into the great world.

What with three or four jobs, theaters, concerts, parties, courtship and marriage to attend to, someone other than my father might have seen the possibilities of becoming a novelist growing more and more remote in the light of the good life he was leading.

Indeed, the legendary background for creating novels was to live for years in a filthy basement on coffee, cigarettes and cheap whiskey. But to my father living in such a way in order to perfect one's writing was about as unrealistic and unhealthy as a Christian martyr going about unwashed and weighting himself with chains to perfect the purity of his love.

Dining, wining, coming to know all sorts of brilliant and ambitious people, and working, among other things, as a "vulgar publicity man" were all a part of the experience it took to make a good story. And, in those hectically wonderful years, he managed somehow to write and discard three novels before presenting what he considered his first book worth publishing to Stokes in 1924. Until that time, no one but my mother had known that he was, in God knows what spare moments, trying to become a novelist.

The result of his years of unpublicized effort was *The Green Bay Tree,* a rich, varied and unified book that caused Mark Sullivan to call him "almost as effective a satirist of his country and generation as Voltaire was of his."

Sullivan was right in saying "almost," for my father would never achieve the depth and scope of that great Frenchman, whom he himself revered. And yet there were some things that Bromfield and Voltaire had in common: Both had a fine sense of balance and humor. Both loved to live fully, taking what life had to offer and making much of it. Neither felt the necessity to suffer and sacrifice all life to writing. Writing was, indeed, an end result, a summation of living. And, after the publication of *The Green Bay Tree,* my father began to live more fully than ever.

He gave up his job with Putnam and began for the first time to depend entirely on his writing for an income. Devoting to it all the time with which he suddenly found himself endowed, he grew enormously productive. Along with countless articles and short stories, he published between 1924 and 1927 four of his finest novels.

He and my mother moved to the relative quiet of Long Island, and there they lived until after the birth of my eldest sister, Anne. Then in 1925 the family went for a short trip to France, during which, one day on a drive through the Oise, they came upon the Presbytère de St. Etienne. They found it in the fading light of an autumn afternoon, its vine-covered walls rising from the narrow, cobblestoned streets of Senlis, its high dormer windows looking out over an ancient stone chapel and a garden of lilacs and poplars, to the green and golden French countryside beyond. The sight of it thus, in the ancient village just before dusk, must have made for them a decision they had long been pondering. For a few days later they returned to take out an eighty-year lease on the Presbytère with the intention of staying, perhaps forever.

The town was far behind my father now and even the memory of the fruitless years spent in universities. Still there must have been moments when, as if waking from a nightmare, relieved and yet a little frightened and indignant at his dream, he realized how near he had come to returning to Ohio from Columbia, thinking, in despair, that after all the world hadn't much more to offer than antimacassars, family reunions and material progress, or, as its only alternative, the sterile confines of academic life.

For sometimes, sitting in the Green Room of an evening, playing backgammon with my mother and listening to the music of some great ballet which made him pause now and then to do a can-can with his fingers on the corked surface of a dilapidated but beautiful old table, he would suddenly shudder as if the very atmosphere of ease and charm about him had brought to mind his narrow escape.

Of Roots and the World

"My God, what if I had allowed myself to be bound and gagged and shut up forever in the front parlor," he would cry. And if my grandmother was in the room, he would address himself to her with a long and meaningful glance, which she inevitably met with a great, voluptuous Wagnerian sigh.

Never were the two more alike than in this moment when they eyed each other full of self-contrived persecution: each one volatile, each one practicing immense humbuggery to produce the proper stage effect. Yet my father always had the greatest difficulty in admitting that he and his mother bore any resemblance to each other. Perhaps his great pride in complete self-reliance would not allow him to concede that it was the very strength and ambition inherited from Ma which had, in the end, pushed him into the world.

If anything might have held him back, it would have been a certain lack of self-confidence, which all his life clung to him like a mantle, invisible to all but those who knew him well; this, coupled with that immense desire to take root and live on the land. But he preferred to pretend that it was Ma who, through her ambition and tremendous possessiveness, had designed to mold his life to suit herself and never allow him to escape from her presence. And, after a time, he came very near to convincing himself that it was no pretense at all, but true.

Thus it was that in *The Green Bay Tree* and *Possession* he depicted his mother as Hattie Tolliver, who by playing the piano for an hour each day before the birth of her daughter wills the girl to become a pianist. Then, with a cruel irony, delightful to the reader, the daughter proves to be stronger and more ambitious than her mother. By marrying a traveling salesman from New York, using him as a steppingstone, she escapes her mother and the town forever to find freedom and fame in the world.

In *A Good Woman,* my grandmother appears again in the character of Emma Downes, who, in her blind determination to build an image of herself and her son walking in the light of

29

supreme Christian rectitude, forces her son to become a Methodist missionary. In the end, having destroyed his health and then his spirit, she manages to preserve the image after his death, becoming the martyred mother of one "who gave his life in Africa bringing heathen souls to God."

A Good Woman was much more viciously exacting in its characters than were the other two novels and was thus probably much more satisfying to readers who like to see their characters realistically crucified. And it was not surprising that we children, having heard Ma discussed from time to time as Emma Downes in the living flesh, regarded our grandmother when she came to visit the Presbytère with mingled suspicion and awe.

I remember her as a heavy but amazingly nimble old woman whose once handsome face now spread and sank over the frame of its still pugnacious jaw, like the face of an aged female bulldog. Her eyes, too, were those of a bulldog. In the midst of all that weatherbeaten belligerence, they shone like two limpid pools of sentiment and sorrow which, when aroused, turned suddenly to fierce, blazing coals.

Her nose was a fascinating replica of the notorious schnozzola of W. C. Fields and had gotten that way, I had been told, as the result of an automobile accident. Ma's nose, as the tale went, had gone through the windshield and been cut "clean off." But Ma, with her great presence of mind, had clapped it on again and held it securely in place until she was taken to a hospital where it could be properly ministered to with needle and thread.

Whenever she drew me—with her great will against my reluctance—onto her ample lap to tell me "sweet little stories," I would sit, oblivious of her kindly, sentimental patter, staring in horrible fascination at her nose and speculating endlessly upon how such a marvelous feat could ever have been accomplished.

There was another story in constant circulation during my childhood, about how Ma had caught her foot in a hole in the carpet at the Hotel Algonquin, plunged down a flight of stairs and broken her hip. Again, with her ever-diligent presence of mind, she had ordered a photo taken of the hole and proceeded to sue for damages. She got nothing for her efforts but a badly mended hip, which caused her gait to be more ungainly than ever, and gave her an excellent excuse to carry a heavy malacca cane. No one ever saw her actually lean on the cane. (Certainly such a concession would have been out of keeping with her character of self-reliance!) But it served as an invaluable aid in separating fighting dogs and, I was also led to believe, in hooking Pa by the throat, whenever his long, aimlessly wandering legs threatened to carry him dangerously out of reach.

All these impressions, originating in our father's mind, which dearly loved to derive fantasy from half truth and then reproduce truth from fantasy, did not help to create in our childish heads a proper respect for the generally venerated state of grandmotherhood. But what of that? Perhaps it helped us to learn to take people as they were, or as we thought they were.

At any rate, whenever I call my grandmother to mind, I still never fail to envision her crashing through the underbrush of our lush and beautiful garden, flailing at the air with her cane in bold pursuit of a pack of squabbling hounds; or clinging to her nose between Forty-fourth Street and New York Hospital; or leaping back in affronted horror as Mr. Gillet, the Curator de Abbaye de Challis, in the most courteous and impeccable French manner, bends to kiss her hand. They are memories I retain with a great feeling of warmth and pleasure. If she had been an ordinary grandmother it is quite possible that I would by now have forgotten her altogether.

Like a child who knows another's vulnerable spots and can't resist prodding them, my father antagonized his mother. He never failed to place her in the honored chair at the foot of the long dining table because he knew that it aggravated her to the point of insanity not to be able to hear, from her great distance, every word he uttered. At cards, he accused her of cheating (often with justification) just to watch the righteous indignation rise and explode like Fourth of July rockets in those sorrowful eyes. Whenever she plunged ahead of him to assert to an admiring stranger with dewy-eyed pride, "I'm Louis's mother," he would come up immediately with a long discourse on how she had discovered him in a basket on the doorstep one morning, and that he was actually the son of a Polish washerwoman and a wandering Armenian cooking-pot salesman.

He regarded Ma with immense distrust always. Pa, whose gentleness and irresolution, had they had no other force to contend with, might easily have held him back, was the recipient of his unending praise and love.

Somehow my sisters and I felt a strange nearness to Pa; perhaps because a long illness had deprived him of his memory and rendered him as dependent, simple and direct as a child. It produced in us feelings at once tender and contrite, for, much as we loved him, his behavior was often the cause of helpless and somewhat heartless mirth.

He was a handsome man, tall and spare with a thick crop of white hair and blue eyes which were like my father's when caught in a moment of gentleness. In another man, as it was in my father, such handsomeness would have been forceful; but in Pa it wasn't, for somehow he was never really there. Instead, a kind of ghost lingered at one's side, its eyes wistfully longing to impart some knowledge born of his long and troubled experience but unable to do so because of the sad, intangible gulf of his lost memory, which held him mute.

And so we remembered him as the childlike ghost who read and quoted despairingly the same newspaper day after day, knowing full well that no one was listening; who, wandering off to rest at night, entered the nursery, climbed into bed with the children and, with the polite "Excuse me" of one who had stumbled into another passenger's reserved seat on a train, wandered off again in the direction of the room he shared with Ma. Lost in Senlis, he often arrived home at dusk, escorted by and carrying on a cheerful conversation in no known language with the butcher, the clothier, the village priest.

Once, on the tail end of a family excursion through the Palace at Versailles, he must have grown exceedingly weary of all the magnificence and pomp of the age of Voltaire and Louis XV, for he disappeared. And when, after a frantic search, we discovered him again, he was on the other side of the velvet rope, seated in a gold-and-damask chair in Madame Pompadour's boudoir, his hands folded peacefully across his spare middle, fast asleep.

My father adored him. If ever he laughed at Pa, which was seldom, there was always a touch of sorrow in his laughter for Pa's helpless plight. When he wrote of him, it was with that magnificent understanding and tenderness (as if it were a part of him too sensitive to be exposed in public, but better left to be read and known by each man in a private moment) he seemed able to impart only through his writing.

He described Pa always as an intelligent, sensitive man who in politics, horse trading and business in general was something of a failure because he hadn't the proper twentieth-century reverence for money and success, but who, in spite of his inability to "see the twentieth-century light" or perhaps because of it, was loved and deeply respected by all.

Oddly enough, it was Pa and not my sturdy, self-sufficient grandmother who made himself at home in France. Perhaps this was because the simple, unassuming atmosphere of Senlis and the solid permanence of its ancient cathedrals and stone walls set amidst the fields and trees brought back to him something of the world he had loved in his youth. In Senlis, an element of self-sufficiency, permanence and peace, which in nineteenth-century America had been but a phase that passed, had been captured long ago and suspended in eternity. And so, in Senlis, probably more than anywhere in his own country, Pa felt at home and at ease.

One day, not long after one of Ma and Pa's turbulent expeditions to France, my father sat down in his quiet shadowy room under the eaves of the Presbytère and began to write a book. It was called simply *The Farm*, and it told the story of his forebears and of the growth and development of the Ohio wild country from the time when the first settlers came into the rich and forested land from beyond the mountains, to the time when the family farm "was sold to a man who bought it as a speculation because now it was within the sound of the mills."

More than anything else, *The Farm* is a description of a way of life so vividly drawn that one can sense the damp, milk and sour smell of the buttery and see the apple butter sputtering like a geyser in its great copper kettle in the cold autumn air. One feels the strength and wisdom of those who knew the richness and hardness of self-sufficient country living and wishes for an injection of that vitality into one's own veins.

In it, my grandfather is James Willingdon, again the ineffectual businessman and politician who was too honest and too indifferent to "success" to play the game of his adversaries. His passion for restoring old, ruined farms inevitably ended in bankruptcy; but nevertheless it taught his children to understand the earth and the countless minute and yet grandly significant happenings connected with it.

"What he gave them," my father wrote in *The Farm*, "was destined to stay with them forever. It was the most precious heritage one could receive. He was a man who knew how to live. He knew the things that count."

My grandmother was again the ambitious, possessive harridan who strove to shape her children's lives even before they were born. But she was also a wonderfully hospitable woman whose house was always alive and full of people; whose "front parlor" was kept open at all times. And in *The Farm*, for her efforts to inspire his curiosity about the world, my father paid her a tribute which in a way atoned for all the "hard words" spent on her in other books. He said, "To her and her vigil Johnny [who was in reality my father] remained eternally grateful for having given him an interest in others rather than in himself."

For my father, I think *The Farm* was a real work of introspection. Sitting in an ancient house in France, so distant from it all, he tried to set down on paper everything he knew of that life he had left behind and weigh his feelings in relation to it. And because of this perhaps he actually believed that he had purged himself at last of any desire ever to return. For, after all, with the final chapter of *The Farm,* he concluded that the nineteenth century, the Ohio wild country and all that it had produced had virtually ceased to exist.

3

The Seasons

Each man has his own version of the meaning of wasted time. To one, it is simply a lack of constructive effort. Still another may say, "Why waste time in creating something when so little of what we make lasts beyond the lifetime of any of us?"

And to this there is another answer still, "But for such a reason should we deprive ourselves of the pleasure of doing what we like?"

With this last I am totally in accord, and I suppose this is so because I was brought up by my father, a man who spent his entire life doing exactly the things that pleased him.

He came to France to discover the world. And the Presbytère de St. Etienne, so rich in its response to his longing for beauty, profundity and continuity, might have halted him—stopped him where he stood—and become the world for him. But his curiosity was as great as his love for the Presbytère. And so the old house, like a mistress who is all the more pleasing for not binding her lover to her, became instead the point of incessant arrivals and departures.

Indeed, his absences, like those of an unreliable lover, from whom word never arrives except by the pen of a mutual and sympathetic friend, were long periods of silence broken only by an occasional brief note from my mother, as enthusiastic and gay as her laughter. Or now and then, an obscene postcard would arrive for Nanny from George, sent principally for the benefit of the postman, who never failed to scrutinize anything that could legally be read.

The arrival of one of those indecent missives would be heralded by robust roars of laughter from up and down Rue St. Etienne, where, as he delivered the mail from door to door, the postman had already provided the neighborhood with its morning laughter. Then, staggering through the kitchen door of the Presbytère, clutching his sides as if better to contain his ribaldry, he would virtually thrust the now dog-eared message into Nanny's morning cup of tea, crying, "Ah, Mon Dieu. Regarde ce qu' arrive pour Mademoiselle à la poste d'aujourd'hui. Ah, mais Monsieur Hookans est vraiment un bonhomme. Regarde bien, Mademoiselle. C'est magnifique, n'est-ce pas?"

But aside from these abrupt notices of their continuing existence, Marco Polo and his entourage could not have been more uninformative about their whereabouts than were my parents until the day when a telegram arrived, heralding their return. The telegram was greeted with as much relief as had been the announcement, not long ago, of their departure. For in a household accustomed to a kind of perpetual chaos in its daily living, the tranquillity of their absence soon became depressing. After a day or two, we were already unadmittedly yet obviously looking forward to the noise and confusion of their return: the descriptions of implausible new friends, the stories, the odd acquisitions which accompanied their messy arrival, from beautiful Venetian lamps to turtles with rubies set in their backs (a gift from the Maharani of Kooch Bahar) to the tiny jewel-eyed mongoose which peeped inquisitively out of my father's coat pocket, where he had made his nest all during the long journey home from Calcutta.

Settled in once more at the Presbytère, my father would tend to his garden, give his upsetting and delightful Sunday lunches and, under the profound and calming influence of the old house, commit his newly acquired discoveries to paper. In this way, he sorted things out and rested a little before he set out to explore the world again.

Generally he and George and my mother set out alone, but during the holiday seasons the entire household often went along: in winter, to the high, snowbound enchantment of the Swiss mountains; in summer, to the rocky sea-worn coast of Brittany. Season after season, we made the same pilgrimage, compelled by a love of familiar places which caused us always to return. The impressions and memories of Europe gained by those constant returnings were as profound as those of the Presbytère, which neither time nor opinions and prejudices of others have ever quite been able to destroy. How we longed for the changing seasons and how we dreamed of them in the silent nights between.

Long before I knew the names of the months, I think I understood the unmistakable signs of approaching winter at the Presbytère. It was heralded by the dry, mysterious odor of moth-balls as Nanny began to shake out, one by one, the skiing costumes, mittens, woolen helmets and heavy socks—her hands trembling with eagerness, her voice complaining with a blatantly false note of bitterness, "Good for the lungs, Madame? Where did you pick up such rot? From *him,* I expect. If you'd like the truth, pure and simple, I'd far rather keep them here and let *him* go traipsing off in all those bitter winds. Hope's such a tiny, miserable little stick and he behaves with her as if she were one of those damnfool ski instructors. Oh no, Madame, I tell you I dread it, simply dread it."

A monologue of this sort was, of course, taken as a certain sign that the excitement of setting off for the winter holiday had reached such a pitch that the possibility of anyone's being left at the Presbytère was purely rhetorical. Hearing it only caused us all to make wild sounds of rejoicing.

Skis appeared next, dusty and as furred with mold as cheese, ripe from the cellars. For days they leaned against the banister in the halls to be waxed and rewaxed and tried by the long, expert finger of my father, who knew so well just how they should be when at last smooth wood touched slippery snow. Boots were lined up and tried on, leather boots and boots of sealskin with metal hooks shining with the expectant cheerfulness that quickly evoked visions of toylike Swiss villages, nestled smug and self-contented, beneath their sugar-frosting of snow.

There are certain things that have a special incomparable excitement about them: Scotch bagpipes, for instance, the sound of a reco-reco in a Brazilian batuque, the smell of maple syrup boiling in an Ohio sugar bush. Because of my father's curiosity and love of life, I have known them all and shall never forget them any more than I shall forget the complete contentment of sitting, warm and secure beneath a great bearskin rug, with the clean, cold snowflakes stinging my face and the tinkling of bells on harnesses accompanied by the heavy thud of the hoofs of powerful Percheron horses, striking the frozen road as our sleigh was drawn through some enchanted snowbound town. At the road's end, in a little hotel, sheltered and warmed against the mountainside, we sat down to hot chocolate and buttered scones held between chilblained fingers and laughed and talked of nothing while a string orchestra dutifully squeaked and struggled to give background to the happiness of our own hearts.

There were only two among us who could call themselves skiers. One was my father, the other that "miserable stick," my sister Hope. She was not more than ten at the time, slight, pale and dreamily delicate. But she had the Bromfield chin, a striking feature which, when photographed from certain angles, resembles the jawpiece of a medieval suit of armor. It was in this feature of my sister's otherwise gentle face that my father, each time they ascended the mountainside, placed whatever confidence he had.

"Look at that chin! How can she do anything but follow it?" he would shout with a strangely hollow heartiness. "That's it! Thrust it forward and keep behind it just the way your grandmother does. Now, are you ready? Push off, then!"

Side by side, they would streak past us down Mount Cellerina, or the treacherous Cordova, a soaring eagle and his near-noon shadow, eyes defiant, chins thrust forward, ski sticks straight behind like the wings of diving birds who know no fear of gravity. At the bottom they would do a fine, simultaneous christy and, turning with a rare display of affection, our father would hug his daughter as if, once again, she had been spared from a fate he'd rather not think about.

In spite of his ill-concealed fear for her safety, he never failed to take Hope back up the mountainside for a repeat performance, and when questioned about the sense of taking such a risk, he would declare with laughing defiance that "After all the honor of the Bromfield jaw was at stake." There was probably more sincerity in that jest than he would have wanted to admit. But beyond that, I believe it was not really in him to resist the pleasure of such grace and prettiness and bravado, flying at his side. He was simply proud of the spirit he had instilled in so apparently flimsy a being.

Just as Hope gave a kind of perfection to his days on the mountainside, George lent a special stimulation to evenings which otherwise, in perpetual expectation of the same faces and the same conversations, might have, after a time, become monotonous.

George, always at his own preconceived height of fashion in any situation, outfitted himself each year at Harrods with handsome skiing costumes that would have excited the dapper senses of the Duke of Windsor himself as they lay in magnificent display across his bed in the Presbytère. But within my admittedly brief memory of George in Switzerland, I recall seeing him garbed in all his sportsmanlike splendor but once. That was on the day when, defiling the pure Swiss air with a choice selection of violent maledictions, he sailed past me, his posterior where his skis should have been, clinging like a drowning man to the dislocated limb of a fir tree. After that, the handsome outfit seemed to have been abandoned to the darkest depths of his closet and, whenever he appeared henceforth, it was in a white toweling bathrobe or a fancy-dress costume.

His hours of daylight in Switzerland were spent cloistered behind drawn curtains with his perpetual sun lamp and scandal sheets that magically turned up wherever he turned up, be it Hollywood, Venice or Gstaad.

And when he was not keeping abreast of calumny the world over, he lay dreaming up costumes and ruminating over what mischief he might create when the sun had left the sky, allowing him to appear (without fear of being wafted off the mountain-tops) for cocktails at seven.

My father may have seemed the embodiment of self-assurance to those who didn't know him. But, in truth, he was a shy man who would never have attempted certain feats without George at his heels to give him the "proper confidence." Still, like George, who needed only to appear in a room for all the company within to begin to nudge one another and grin, the Boss (as he was offhandedly referred to by his manager through all their years together) craved laughter. And so, with George at his side, countless comical and often perilous schemes were hatched which otherwise might never have gotten past the stage of being amusing brainstorms.

There was, for example, a day in Paris when, elbowing their way through an agitated crowd, the pair conceived the idea of wrenching two banners from the hands of their astonished bearers and marching through a Communist rally bellowing, "Vive la Monarchie, Démocratie et J. P. Morgan!"

Greeted with a scattering of "merdes" and a good deal of hearty French laughter, they survived this gallant spearhead for

democracy to carry out an ingenious smuggling act, the successful mechanics of which no one (including the management of
the swank Hotel George V) has ever been able to discover. All
that is known is that when their good friends Gene and Spike
Mixsell returned to their suite from an evening of dinner and
dancing they discovered a large duck swimming contentedly in
the bathtub and the Presbytère de St. Etienne's most elegant
game cock perched in attendance on the towel rack (malheureuse-
ment) making droppings everywhere.

In India they had appeared at an elegant dinner for the
British Consul, dressed in tuxedos with their shirttails hanging
out in proper Hindu tradition. And not long afterward, in that
same exotic land, they had joined a strange procession of
chanting, dancing Moslems in anticipation of some exciting fete,
only to discover themselves, after miles of hot, dusty mystic
gyrations, being led through the gates of Calcutta's leprosarium.

In Switzerland, the holiday spirit only heightened their delight
in the ridiculous, so that one evening they might dress as mountain boys and appear for dinner in Tyrolean hats, knee socks,
suitably rotten, greasy mountaineers' shorts and large red, false
noses; another, as Baby Buntings in lace bonnets and long white
nightgowns. And more than once they partook so enthusiastically
of Swiss festive concoctions that they had to be dosed personally
and not a little vindictively with castor oil by the hotel manager himself.

Their capacity for drinking others under the table was better
developed than their ability to overeat and remain unaffected.
By the end of an evening of consuming a more than liberal
quantity of martinis or manhattans, they managed still to continue as perpendicular masters of their own destinies, a state
of being which provided them considerable leverage over those
around them.

So it happened one evening in Arosa when everyone had attained that hard-to-reach state of mellowness prescribed in

Christian teachings, wherein all the world is one, that a young lady in a desperate moment approached George and, in the unabashed language of the period, bellowed at him, "Where's the can?"

Looking into her eyes, which regarded him with implicit if myopic trust, he smiled accommodatingly and motioned toward a door behind him, "Of course—right through there." Laying his hand on the knob with expert continental deference, my father, who had been standing close by, swept the door open for the lady, who, already wrestling with the placket of her ski pants, backed through to the sound of explosive laughter and shouts of "bravo!"

Imagine for yourself her sobering sensations when instead of the "can" she discovered that she had prepared to seat herself on a backward-thrust number-four ball, about to be spun down the center of the Hotel Arosa's bowling alley.

There is one more tale to be told before moving on from the hilarity of winter to the relative tranquillity of summer. It happened in St. Moritz in 1935 and had to do with a well-known young French playwright and his equally well-known mistress. They were an extremely quarrelsome pair. Each time an argument erupted, they packed up separately and sent their luggage (some forty pieces) down to the station to be shipped off to Paris on the afternoon train. But by the time the train had arrived, the lovers' wrangle had come to a sweet halt and back would come the luggage accompanied by the most harassed valet and hysterical maid on the Continent.

For a week the Boss and George watched with great restraint this shuttling back and forth, which resembled the movement of an armored division, up and down the elevator of the Hotel St. Moritz. At last, on the fourth appearance of the increasingly battered-looking entourage, they could no longer resist the obvious move. While George detained the valet with sympathetic conversation and a drink at the bar, my father rushed as fast as his long legs could carry him down to the station with special orders from "Monsieur and Madame" that the luggage was to be dispatched immediately on the train which was leaving for Schaffhausen on the Swiss-German border.

The removal was all the more effective because Madame, expecting the return of her trunks by 2 P.M. as usual, had remained with nothing but a peignoir of the most delicate Parisian satin, and Monsieur with a silk dressing gown with a large dragon embroidered across the back, extremely handsome but somewhat inappropriate for winter sports.

We went to Switzerland for the winter season not only because of my father's love of skiing and the cold enchantment of the Swiss mountains, but because it was the fashionable thing to do. Everyone was there: rich Indian princes, shahs and begums, all of titled Europe and moneyed America. There were the accomplished, rich, brilliant and jaded "international white trash" of whom he wrote in "Deluxe," *The Man Who Had Everything*, "The Listener" and "Death in Monte Carlo." In his descriptions, they hurried back and forth across the face of Europe in constant pursuit of the seasons, of company, of pleasure, notoriety, love and—sometimes—of reality, which in the artificiality of their lives so often eluded them.

He knew them well and wrote of them with both irony and compassion. He understood their basic humanity, which often became (as he saw it) smothered in the scramble for success, or suffocated by excessive wealth and privilege which had never allowed them to breathe the exhilarating air of a hard struggle.

A part of him belonged to them, for he loved them, enjoyed their smartly sophisticated conversation, and was enchanted still by the brilliance of a world of which he had dreamed ever since, long ago, those tempting novels had slipped from his mother's designing hands into his own. But another part of him belonged solely to himself: a certain anchoring strength which must be a part of any man lucky enough to so love his profession that, if life itself seems not to have any particular reason, at least living has an object.

That object is something which caused my father to rise each morning and with eagerness greet the day, if only for the purpose of sitting down at the end of it to choose those moments worth dwelling upon and record them with pleasure and wonder. It was that anchoring strength which prevented him from following the crowd in the summer season; which made the weather-creased face and latent thoughts of a Brittany fisherman as meaningful to him as the tragic brilliance of the Barrymores and the charm and wistful elegance of Lady Patricia Ward. And so, in summer, we departed from the general course of the "international white trash" and searched for such hidden places as Rospico, Pont Manec, St. Cast, Concarneau.

Instead of the great speed with which we set off for Switzerland so as not to miss a single day's skiing or a single gala evening, we took our time in going to Brittany. Somehow we sensed that the summer in the sea wind that lay waiting for us tolerated no impatience, no hurry. Each moment was to be accepted as it came and lived fully. And in the end, it seemed, it was this train of small intimate pleasures, taken like short sips of good wine, that won for us over the impatiently awaited, much acclaimed and always slightly disappointing pleasures of the crowded, spectacular winter.

Of all those winter sports, perhaps only the flight down a mountainside could compare with the countless small excitements of summer in Brittany. And that, I am sure, was because the flight, like the hauling in of a weighted line at sea, was a simple reality of nature: the one made possible by wind and snow on a mountainside, the other by the strange, timeless wizardry of the sea. Both reassured us that we were not, after all, entirely in charge of our own fate. And that, to human nature—always appalled at the weight of final decisions—is a comforting thought, one which my father continually led us back to by exposing all our senses to the only true miracles—those that begin and end with earth and universe. So, in pursuit of proof of our human frailty, we squashed ourselves, along with luggage, dogs, sometimes even cats and canaries, into a sagging vintage station wagon and made our ponderous way toward the sea.

The station wagon had been a gift from my godmother, Beth Leary, a New York heiress with the decided tastes and habits of a migratory bird, who spent all her springs in Paris, and all her spring Sundays at the Presbytère. Upon reception, my father had delightedly named the station wagon La Beth in her honor, painting the title in bold red letters across the left front door.

With time, the surrounding varnish had peeled away, but the red letters remained bright as ever. And for many years the sight of La Beth pulling up before some quiet country inn in Brittany was as sure a sign of coming summer as the arrival of Beth Leary at the Ritz in Paris was a sign which hailed the spring.

Wherever night found us, we stopped to rest. Perhaps it was Lavalle, where, after a good French country dinner, we children with Nanny would climb an ancient stone stairway to sink gratefully into one immense welcoming feather bed, ample for the four of us. In the freshness of dawn, we rose again and moved on so that by evening of the next day we had reached our destination: an old, circular fort at Pont Manec; an aged villa hidden among live oaks at Rospico; a house with a magnificent view at Concarneau.

The view always settled it. Once my father had discovered a view, plumbing, lighting, roofing, all other conveniences or lack of them were superfluous. What did it matter if, when it rained, all the cooking pots and basins in Brittany set side by side could not provide us with an inch of dry floor? Little tributaries emerged from mysterious headwaters in the ceiling and ended in closets, the doors of which one opened with deliberate caution for fear of being struck in the chest by the object of one's search-

Sunday lunch at the Presbytère: (r. to 1.) Charles Bromfield, Ina Claire, Leslie
Howard, Mary Bromfield—others unidentified.

Presbytère de St. Etienne, Senlis, France, 1935.

Louis Bromfield at his writing desk at Senlis.

George Hawkins and
Nanny (Jeanne White) at
the photographers, Senlis.

The Bromfield family at Senlis: (r. to l.) Anne, Hope, Louis, Mary, and Ellen.

Louis Bromfield and Mary Bromfield, Anne, and Nanny (Jeanne White) in France.

George Hawkins and Louis Bromfield after a successful tiger hunt as guests of the Maharaja of Baroda, India, 1933.

"The Three Witches."

Bromfield as an ambulance
driver for the French Army,
World War I.

Ma (Annette) Bromfield at Senlis,
1935.

Above, left, Gene Mixsell; above, right, Beth Leary; right, Annie Chamay.

Louis Bromfield and Edna Ferber on the beach in Brittany, France.

(L. to r.) Hope, Ellen, and Anne in the garden at the Presbytère.

ing as it rushed out on the flood tide.

But rain came seldom and, in its absence, we were inclined to agree with the Boss on his conception of superfluity. For from the terrace of some old house in which the scent and sound of the sea were imprisoned as in a conch shell we could look out over the orange-tiled roofs of the town each evening toward a sun-laden sea.

There, before night fell, a hundred fishing smacks with red and blue sails, some floating regretfully high, others deep in the water with their burden of glistening silver tuna, made their way toward the shore. At first, they were distant specks on a curved horizon, and then each became singular and brilliant, outlined in the last blaze of sunlight before they seemed to dissolve like phantoms and become one with the lapping waters.

My mother spent most of her summers on one little terrace or another, shaded by tall poplars and live oaks, bent seaward by the wind. She sat reading the latest novels sent on from Paris and London and watching and waiting (as had become her incessant role in life) for our return from the scene which lay below her—the cliffs and dunes and Norman sea.

Down on the beach, my eldest sister, Anne, wandered alone with her all-encompassing curiosity, scrutinizing and collecting fragments of sea life. Every rock, shell, fossil, and bit of kelp was a point of endless fascination to her. And if my mother had not, from time to time, nervously called her back, I often think she might be wandering those beaches still—needless of company, oblivious of time—imagining, pondering, discussing with herself the place of each fragment in the scheme of everything.

There was in Brittany something to satisfy each of us—even George, who exchanged his sun lamp for the true light of Helios and lay all day on the sands like an overfed lobster washed ashore by the tide.

For the rest of us, it was the sea itself. At cold predawn, while the mist still clung eerily to all the earth and waters, we hurried to the surf to seek our friend, the Brittany fisherman.

We found him, a small and wizened man, his face massed with wrinkles, his expression astringent from numberless seasons of salting. The web of wrinkles that covered his face showed him to be in latter years and yet his wiriness belied his age, so that looking at him one felt that the true secret of youth must somehow be bound up with battling the sea.

Doffing his grimy cap to the Boss and chuckling (for he knew a good fisherman when he saw one), he would bend toward the ropes that bound his little skiff. And, in a little while all of us, with the dogs centered nervously in the bow, would be drifting out toward dawn and deep water.

One might have thought that for the purpose of gaining the greatest ascetic value from his days at sea the Boss would have set out alone with the old Breton and his battered, fish-smelling craft. But the Boss was perhaps the shyest of all with those he most admired, and undoubtedly the thought of being alone, observing and being observed, with the old man would have caused in the end miserable discomfort for them both. Better to make it expansive, noisy and impersonal. Then, too, the complications aroused by our presence must have held a certain fascination for my father. For in spite of incessant groaning protestations—"My God, what martyrdom to be as I am, surrounded forever by fools and idiots!"—he never failed to take us along.

The need to leap in and break up a raging battle between dogs and spider crabs in the bottom of the boat caused just the right stimulation when—if the truth be known—things had begun to get plain boring. And nothing delighted him more, when Nanny and I turned colicky with the ocean roll, than to photograph from every angle our miserable green pallor as we lay back— suppressing our urges—among the canvases and fish heads in the bow.

On days when we were all happily unnauseated, he watched

48

with satisfaction and even joined in our scramble from one side of the boat to the other as we fell over one another to catch sight of the murky flutter of a school of mackerel or herring close to the surface. And when at last he'd had enough of our rowdiness and really craved silence, he had only to shout in a voice that no one would care to contest, "Quiet down before I beat the bejesus out of the lot of you!" for things to fall as silent as the inside of King Tut's tomb.

Nor did it seem burdensome, this suddenly imposed quiet, which allowed us to gain the full physical pleasure from our stillness in the sun, wind and salt spray. Sometimes in the midst of it, my father could be seen watching the old man who tended the rudder with a strange look of envy and admiration. He loved the fisherman for his strength, which defied all weather and all hardship and was certainly composed of something deeper and more enduring than the mere physical power of his scrawny body. His envy of the old man and all the old men of Brittany arose, I think, from the thought of their peace of mind. For by their daily contact with the sea, which is older than life itself, they had come to know a great many truths which others, searching over the earth for a lifetime, might never discover. And if they could not express what they knew in their coarse, spare language, it mattered little, for it was written in their faces, as deeply grained as old wood, which showed simplicity, pride and humility and a strange but credible combination of fatalism and self-reliance. They were content with things as they were. And, although it was not in my father's nature to endure contentment for long, I believe he would happily, for a day or two, have exchanged his soul for that of a Brittany fisherman in order to experience its total peace.

There was, by the end of all our summers in Brittany, scarcely a cliff or a landslide of boulders, halted in their tumble toward the sea by the same force of gravity that had set them loose, that we had not explored. Nor was there a lonely beach with whose incoming tide we were not on the most familiar and trusting terms.

We were like a tireless flock of brown goats with a great clever and mischievous he-goat as our leader, scampering barefooted over the endless rocky coast, reeling on the edges of boulders, our toes wet by the treacherous sea spray, our ears deafened by the violent roar below. At our father's bidding, we disappeared into cool, hidden crevices. At Nanny's tormented shrieks, we sprang out again in wicked glee and ran ahead, bold in the certainty that Nanny could bleat all she liked; for the more daring were our exploits, the more roundly they suited the old he-goat's pleasure.

Exhausted at last, we would find a place where the tide had polished and scooped out a hollow pool in some great, aged rock. Sitting with our toes in its sunlit waters and our backs against the warm boulders, we would stay for hours watching the scurry of sea life, lifted up, so it seemed, and placed in this shallow bowl for just such lovingly prodigious wasters of time as we.

Presently, growing weary again of sitting still, we would descend to the beach and willingly submit ourselves to the slavery of carrying water for the building of Mont-Saint-Michel or some medieval castle out of sand. We would race with crazed energy to finish the conglomeration of turrets, battlements, balconies and bridges in time for the tide to pour with tragic portent over the walls of the moat. And when we had finished, we would sit in a row on the sands, watching with delicious, horrid fascination the excavation of the dungeons, the wearing away of the torture chambers, ballrooms and dining hall. While we watched, the sky above us faded from intense blue to the pale iridescence that accompanies the coral red of sunset, low against the sea. The fishing smacks sailed out of the setting sun and the moon appeared in the pale sky—hesitant, like an actress ahead of her cue—before we, with the ravenous hunger of sea-farers, turned at last toward a distant light in the hill.

Late at night, when the stars were like jewels fastened to a great black mantle suspended benignly over all Brittany, my father sat at a card table covered with papers, by a window high above the sea. Watching the moon, now bold in the darkness, on her path across the waters, and listening to the stillness, his thoughts might have been of Annie Spragg, whose ironic, lonely tale was of the stuff that myths and saints are made. Or of Lilli Barr, who knew too well where she was bound; or of someone he had met in Venice during another season, whom he was about to depict as the rich, hard and sensual Princess d'Orebelli.

They were all his characters, drawn from his knowledge of a vast and complex world of which he tried his best never to allow any part to escape his vision. And after an afternoon spent on the edge of a rock pool and in the "useless pleasure" of building castles in the sand, I believe he saw them with a greater clarity and imagination than ever so that on paper they glowed with an eccentric brilliance that made them more credible and more alive.

With a kind of new excitement about life, he wrote until daylight, knowing as he did that the moment in the sun had passed, the castle had dissolved into sand again as all things we make must do, so that nothing is left in the end but the earth and the thoughts we leave behind us.

Like the castle, like a house built or a garden made, his writing might one day disappear as if it had never existed. I doubt if the Boss gave it much thought. There wasn't time. For during his brief stay amidst the unfathomable pattern of life as it was, he had long ago decided to hurry on, living and working and doing exactly as he liked.

4

The Garden and the Pattern

"I knew that the hardest thing for me to bear in leaving France and Europe was not the loss of the intellectual life I had known there, nor the curious special freedom a foreigner knows in a country he loves, nor the good food, nor even the friends I would be leaving behind. The thing I should miss most, the thing to which I was most attached were the old house and the few acres of land spread along the banks of a little river called the Nonnette. . . . If I never saw it again a part of my heart would always be there in the earth, the old walls, the trees and vines I had planted, in the friendships that piece of earth had brought me. . . ."

L. B.

On the side facing east, where the sun's first and friendliest rays shone through faded green shutters, the Presbytère de St. Etienne rose straight up like a lime cliff out of the waters of a canal called La Nonnette.

La Nonnette, the Little Nun, flowed through fields of sun-yellowed wheat, speckled with blue cornflowers and brilliant red Flanders poppies; through cool, dark forests and aged villages which had partaken of her waters since the time of the Gauls. There were, indeed, so many places and creatures blessed by La Nonnette that one couldn't help feeling, upon looking into her silent, confident waters, that she knew, like a little old nun whose brain contained the confessions of hundreds of lifetimes, a great deal of what went on in the world. She must have known the scandals of the petite noblesse, scattered across her waters with the vindictive suds of red-armed washerwomen, and the confessions of lovers who used her bridges as settings for their minutely planned and haphazardly executed scenes. She must have sensed the love of the black-bearded Arab Spahis for their horses as they bathed them in the river, cursing them harshly and stroking them gently while the handsome beasts nuzzled the coolness of her waters. And surely she must have understood all about my father and his passionate love for his garden.

For where her banks ceased to give rise to the walls of the Presbytère, they supported another low wall of gray stone atop which stood great pots of geraniums and fuchsias and ageratum, whose drooping flowers hung on woody stems to the very edge of the water. Beyond this wall, the black, fertile earth of the banks of the Nonnette were massed with phlox, pinks, giant delphiniums, foxglove and all varieties of lilies, slender and gay, which turned in the breeze that swept her current softly along.

Across the Nonnette, a small wooden bridge, covered with roses which in midsummer hung in a curtain of tight fragrant blossoms as lush and impenetrable as jungle vine, joined one side of the garden with the other. An orchard of apples and pears stood along her left bank, and in the shadow of the old trees grass grew in a thick carpet through which violets and daffodils forced their way in the spring, while in the patches of sun, light, gay, mouse-faced pansies, alyssum and chrysanthemums grew, sturdy and heavy with blooms.

On the opposite side of the Nonnette, tall poplars rose straight upward to the intense blue of the sky and, at their knees, the French lilacs gave forth heavy, deep purple blossoms, the fragrance of which filled the garden and stole in through the high doors of the Presbytère, which were thrown open to catch their scent and all the scents of earth opening in the spring.

The whole was surrounded by a high stone wall, gray and damp and seamed in its crevices with moss and ivy, atop which Ricky Ticky Tavy, our mongoose, took his morning egg while a flock of white fantailed pigeons strutted and quarreled and flew off to feed their screaming young in nests among the beams of the chapel which stood at the wall's end.

The chapel was older than the Presbytère by four centuries and had retired long ago from its worshiping. And yet it had never quite given up its holiness, not even when my father set energetically to work digging up its earthen floor to convert it into a hothouse.

We children helped with the digging and before long we discovered bones which the Boss excitedly concluded must have been those of ancient Gauls buried at the time those people were hiding from invading Romans in the eerie subterranean passages which wound their secret ways from one old house to another in Senlis. I have never forgotten the sight nor the feel of those bones: brittle and powdery and orange as wood fungus with their great age—fascinating, horrid and romantic to touch.

My father, somewhat irreverently perhaps, worked the bones back into the rich black earth with a bit of chicken manure and planted among them the first flowers to be set out in the warm, thaw-scented days of winter's end. He felt no qualms about thus treating consecrated ground. How could he? For nothing was nearer to his conception of God than the cycle in nature which begins with birth and ends with rebirth. And so, by planting spring flowers among the bones of ancient Gauls, he was simply bringing about a certain harmony which man, in his harsh, pedantic, supposedly Christian thinking and preaching, often manages to destroy. Perhaps it is wrong to feel thus: that man should not consider himself on a higher level than the earth and plants and beasts which he makes his instruments. But I believe my father was right. The happiest people I know are those who love and respect just such things. And I think

54

the holiest chapel I have ever entered was that one at the end of the garden of the Presbytère. About it there was a damp, clean smell of fresh earth, and the deep silence within was disturbed only by the squabbling of the pigeons high up among the rafters. And through the opaque, dust-coated windows the sun shone with a strange, gentle benevolence, as if heaven approved of the first hint of spring greenness in the damp earth of the floor below. We worked silently and happily, enveloped by a sensation of peace and the rightness of things.

I think this sensation of well-being which came to him in the garden was perhaps the only real peace my father ever knew. I can't say exactly why it had this effect upon him. I only know that often when he was in a black mood of the kind which made it most desirable to avoid him at any cost he had only to go into the garden to put things right again. Watching him from a distance as he worked among his flowers in the chapel or beside La Nonnette, one could almost see the calm come over him.

Sometimes, he simply stretched out on the grass and fell asleep. And, more often than not, it was Ricky the mongoose who awakened him, leaping with the agility of a killer of snakes onto his back; or, with a morbid Far Eastern sense of humor, dragging a recently murdered mouse the length of his master's sleeping body to deposit it deftly on the back of the Boss's neck. The little mongoose would then retreat to a respectable distance and wait for the spine-chilling sensation to bring my father back from the distant realms of unconsciousness. Then, as the big man sat bold upright and shuddering, he would leap into his lap to receive with wicked self-indulgence a shower of somewhat undeserved loving caresses and praise. When Ricky had been sufficiently flattered, he was dismissed with a tap and a suggestion that he take his mouse and bury it, and my father would take up his trowel and set to work.

It was as if, absorbed in the business of dividing lilies, his thoughts rearranged themselves without his knowledge; as if new ideas came to him like the circles which arose on the waters of La Nonnette from something beneath the surface, alive and unseen. At any rate, the transformation was so impressive that we often found ourselves wishing only that he might have gone out to the garden a bit earlier.

Still, as it was, we blessed the garden for its magical effect, which, in the end, I suppose arose simply from the things Pa had taught my father as a boy about oneness with the whole pattern of earth and universe and life itself. Certainly this idea became so important to him as time went by that it became a sort of religion; the center of his beliefs. And even though his own ego would never allow him to lose himself in the pattern for long, his faith in its meaning was so great that the measure of happiness attributed to the characters in his stories was inevitably gauged by their ability to understand and become a part of it themselves.

Those who through greed or fear of deprivation betrayed within themselves such things as courage, integrity and kindness —the Tom Dantrys and Edwina Eskeths and Princess d'Orebellis of his Indian and Italian stories—he condemned with Michelet's sad phrase: "Dans la damnation le feu est la moindre chose: supplice propre ou damné est le progrès infini dans le vice et le crime, l'âme s'endurcissent, se dépravant . . . dans le mal de la minute en progression géométrique pendant l'éternité."

Somehow, in losing these principles, they had lost contact with the pattern of life as well, and without it no basic happiness could ever be regained.

Others, who through unbroken ties with the land and deep roots in tradition, understood the meaning of a simplicity which had nothing to do with dullness or naïveté but with the ability to sort out things of value and live thus, without fear or greed, were the happy ones. Among these were Elaine, the handsome French farm wife in *The Man Who Had Everything* and the old Maharani of *The Rains Came*. In reality, the old Indian woman was the Maharani of Baroda, whom my father had met on his first trip to India. She came often to Paris and on Sundays used to drive in her lavender-colored Rolls-Royce to Senlis for the regular Sunday lunches. A tiny woman no more than five feet tall, clothed in gold-embroidered silk saris and fabulous emeralds and walking with the gait of a true queen, she commanded the complete attention of everyone about her wherever she went. When the boisterous afternoon had come to an end and most of the guests had departed it often pleased her to sit in the Red Room amidst the fantastic jungle scenes of her country and indulge in a game of poker.

From beginning to end the game was something of a frantic test of wits. The Maharani liked not only to play a hard game; she felt it a royal prerogative to win. It was necessary, therefore, to select players who could play poker in reverse; who could bluff to lose, rather than to win. A fairly simple game became thus as intricate and abstract as Far Eastern philosophy. And all this was further complicated by the necessity to avoid the old lady's gaze; for one look from the burning, amber eyes of the Maharani of Baroda caused all attempt at duplicity to dissolve into ineffectuality. My father always swore that when she regarded you she seemed to be remembering all the lies you had told since your mother caught you with an empty candy box sixty or seventy years ago.

And still, among his happiest moments were those spent in getting up a poker game for the Maharani. She was everything my father loved and respected. She was elegant and queenly, and at the same time earthy and direct in her manner, and full of quick, subtle humor. She knew what was valuable in life and could be calmly ruthless and tyrannical when she felt her values needed defending. In all her make-up she had the wisdom and courage of one who is born to lead people.

Certainly that wonderful old Indian woman, who was the most important character in *The Rains Came*, and Elaine, the French

farmer's wife of *The Man Who Had Everything* were for my
father a part of the pattern. They saw themselves as part of the
design of birth, death, rebirth, and the continuity, from one life
to the next, of earth and human ideas. And in their images were
gathered all his highest ideals.

But just as every writer writes of things in which he believes,
so does he tend to judge the power of others to achieve them by
what he believes his own abilities to be. And so when my father
wrote of Tom and Elaine in *The Man Who Had Everything*,
I think he must have seen a great deal of himself in the well-
known playwright who, bored at times to near insanity by the
world full of "nothing but successful people" in which he lived,
could never quite bring himself to exchange it for the un-
notorious yet more deeply satisfying life of Elaine, whom he
loved.

This world of nothing but successful people was not my
father's only world. And yet, even if he had found it to be as
completely banal as he often described it in his books, he could
never have renounced it. For he was, in truth, no more immune
to the American preoccupation with success than was *The Man
Who Had Everything*. The need to exist always at the height
of everything that was fashionable and recognized fascinated and
tormented him. And always, in the end, it drove him to the
garden where he could seek out "the pattern" at odd moments
beneath the shadow of an ancient chapel on the edge of the
Nonnette.

He had a gardener named Piquet, a strong, red-skinned peasant
who, much to my grandmother's disgust, wrapped his stomach
in yards of seldom-changed flannel both winter and summer
(contre la grippe) and who had a French peasant's shrewdness
and earthy sense of humor.

When first he came to work at the Presbytère, Piquet thought
my father to be one of those pests who, though never having
handled a spade, would constantly butt in with orders that upset

everything just as the delicate balance of gardening had begun to work its magic. But before long he discovered how wrong he had been and came to respect the Boss for that instinctive reverence for earth which was as strong in him as in any good French peasant.

Together, the two worked long hours, bending over the soil with spades and watering the plants with an odoriferous brew of chicken manure water, ripened, like wine, in the chapel's old wells. They worked in silence, enjoying the sun on their backs and the smell and sight of things which both of them, in spite of the separate worlds in which they lived, loved with exactly the same fervor. And when they did speak to each other, their talk arose as naturally as a cool breeze comes up in the fields on a hot summer day, coming neither from aggravation nor politeness, but from a simple desire to stir the still air about them for a while with their thoughts.

Sometimes they talked of politics, my father questioning and curious; Piquet, stubbornly assured and instinctively right in his peasant's certainty that no social benefit proffered by this or that politician of the day was half so precious as the small plot of land which was his security and independence—his possession.

They loved to observe together, and to respond with the ribald humor that had once so tickled M. Rabelais and M. Balzac, the constant, unstaged drama that went on all about them in the village. They wailed and shook convulsively over the sorry fate of Piquet's uncle, who, having resolved to marry his woman after eighteen years and fourteen children, indulged in a drunken tussle with his future brother-in-law on his wedding day, was kicked in the stomach and promptly expired.

They chuckled delightedly as they contemplated from the sanctuary of the lilacs the village jeweler, M. Printemps, a pompous, "pious" and unscrupulous being, scurrying across the bridge minus the seat of his pants with our Scottie, Dash, in earnest pursuit. And nothing gave them greater pleasure than to watch from the hidden vantage point the progress of the little one-armed postman, who took a glass of wine at every house where he stopped to deliver the mail and, at his leisure, read the postcards. How they loved him and laughed with him as he reeled down the Rue Presbytère and into our kitchen for a Cointreau at the end of the line.

After many years of carrying out this precarious expedition daily, the little postman was fired for losing letters along the way. Jobless, crippled and hopeless, he somehow managed to hang himself. Piquet's and my father's outrage and sorrow at the incident were unanimous and enormous. And ever afterward, they could never quite reconcile themselves to the appalling emptiness that replaced that well-meaning, tipsy, laughable breath of life. "All," they would shake their heads together and say, "for the loss of a few letters."

The two, as they worked side by side, stopped to rest and talk and laugh a little, or look with despondency upon the tragedies of life, and found themselves in agreement over a great many things which reached far beyond their love of flowers. And the thoughts of Piquet remained strong in my father's mind long after a great many "intellectual" discussions had faded from lack of reality and meaning.

But in all the years that they knew one another, in all their experiences together, I think my father's devotion to Piquet became amaranthine on the day that his flannel-swathed friend made him the perplexed recipient of an enormous black puppy whose head seemed to have been reduced hideously by some ancient African formula. The pup, Piquet declared with the confidence of one who recognizes good breeding when he sees it, was the offspring of his own German police bitch and our admittedly tenacious Dash.

On that day, for the first time in their long acquaintance, my father regarded Piquet with something of doubt.

"Mais, Piquet, vous voyez, vous-même, c'est impossible, absolument impossible. . . ."

Piquet, who, with his French common sense, believed no more in miracles than the Boss, drew himself up at this uncalled-for aspersion on his credibility and squelched the doubt with a neat finality.

"N'est pas possible, hein? Pardon, Monsieur, mais rien n'est impossible. Naturellement, j'ai aidé un peu," said he, stroking the outcome of his and Dash's combined efforts with a proud and accomplished hand.

This story became the favorite tale at the Ritz in Paris for months and was later translated into ten languages for all the world to read.

And so the garden, La Nonnette and the village which surrounded them provided not only solidity and peace but a setting for the making of great and lasting friendships, the scene of tragedies and comedies and all the wonderful ironic and amusing aspects of humanity.

Carnivals came to town with sword swallowers and merry-go-rounds and a shooting gallery, the bull's eye of which once inadvertently forced the lock on a swinging door that flew open to reveal a fat, jolly belle dame, seated with a look of amiable ribaldry on the loo.

Once a year, the Arab Spahis, who came from nearby Chantilly to bathe their horses in La Nonnette, gave an exhibition in the autumn-brown fields outside the village. Dressed in full regalia of billowing white pants, turbans and red tunics, with flashing sabers at their sides, they jumped their magnificent horses through flaming hoops and over tables covered with glasses of wine.

And in between times, just when the air of the village seemed to be becoming overladen with recumbent tranquillity, the rubber factory, housed within the relic of a sixteenth-century hotel across the street, erupted with the explosion of one piece or another of its only slightly more youthful machinery.

Whenever this occurred, our kitchen door was immediately flung open to a swarm of screaming, weeping factory girls and a flurry of nuns from Le Sacré Coeur, who hurried forth to staunch the wounds. Happily, the wounds were always more Gallicly dramatic than painful, and once the last scratch was safely daubed and bound, the nuns would seat themselves around the long blackened and scarred kitchen table for a cup of tea.

I often think of my father as rather welcoming those volcanic sounds from across the street for the rare opportunity they afforded him of a talk with La Mère Supérieure. For not only was she most beautiful to look upon, her stiff white habit only serving to accentuate the fineness of the handsome features which it framed; she was neither shy nor tormented and bitter as nuns often become as a result of their self-effacing lives. My father told us this was so because she had joined the order of Le Sacré Coeur neither from loneliness nor rejection of her fellow men but out of a simple, truthful desire to become a nun. He always claimed this simple manner of choosing one's profession to be at the bottom of any great success, be it that of a financial magnate or an artist or a religieuse. He didn't believe in self-retribution for its own sake and about this he and La Mère Supérieure were capable of arguing a whole morning if only time permitted it.

"You can't tell me," he would begin, once he was seated in an elevated position on a high kitchen stool, "that all those penitents are suffering for the sins of humanity. If you want to know, it strikes me they're suffering because they like it."

La Mère Supérieure would remain unruffled. Only a faint but all the same distinct inward smile would seem to hint that she was perhaps considering any number of penitents who gave solid grounds for the Boss's point of view.

"Don't discount penitents with such dispatch, Monsieur. The

sins of the world are a great burden."

"All the more reason, Mère Supérieure, to spread it around; let each man carry his own share. Don't you really think that's more sensible than running to the church once a week and heaping it all on the shoulders of one poor overworked priest, who has enough to do as it is without worrying about other people's bad behavior?"

"The priest is God's envoy, Monsieur Bromfield. It is through him that all people suffer onto the Lord."

"Aha!" My father would just miss toppling his stool in delight. "Just what I wanted to hear from you! Then you agree, Reverend Mother, that God hasn't enough time in the day to listen to all our petty troubles? For what other reason would He have given us the Ten Commandments to follow on our own? Come now. You must often have thought as I have that when a man acts against one of these commandments he must suffer more within himself when there is no one to tell, no punishment to relieve him of his sins?"

If my father felt that he had by now gained the upper hand, he should have been more wary of the latent twinkle in the elderly nun's eye, the laugh all within herself that must have said, "You think you have conquered me and made me show my hand, but I can be as insidious as you and the battle has just begun."

"Ah, Monsieur," she would sigh defeatedly, "you are quick with your questions and sharp with your reasoning. You leave me standing almost without defense. But, as you know your own soul so well, perhaps you can tell me the number of times you have rationalized over your own errors and made up a new rule to justify them. No, Monsieur Bromfield, there was but one man on earth who did not need a father all his life, someone to set an example and mete out a punishment from time to time. Take yourself, for example. If I may be so bold, I have often heard it said, Monsieur, that you are incapable of speaking a paragraph without taking our Lord's name in vain (Commandment Number 2). Yet, *I*, for one, have never heard a curse from your lips. Would it be possible, Monsieur Bromfield, that my habit has some sort of restraining effect upon your normally unbridled tongue?"

With a calculatedly nonchalant shrug, my father would counter, "Deference, Mère Supérieure; I have a great respect for others' convictions, even if at times I find them warped." But from the heightening of color and the unmistakably foolish grin on his face, it was obvious that he had been nailed; that from here on his retreat would be as spectacular as La Mère Supérieure's advance, until at last they stood on a common ground which looked so peaceful and full of accord that one could not help feeling that perhaps the two worlds for which they spoke were not half as far apart as they seemed.

After too short a time, for she was always far too busy to indulge for long in philosophies with Le Fou Americain, La Mère Supérieure would gather her flock of little nuns about her and take her leave. From the kitchen window, my father would watch their dainty, gliding procession until all were out of sight. Then smiling in a special way reserved for those moments when humanity aroused in him a restoration of faith, he would say, "She is magnificent. A great lady, so grand, so dignified and human. It's a good thing, by God, that some of her sort belong to the Church to keep them from crucifying the rest of us."

And then he would walk out into the garden, his head full of questions about the Catholic Church that might never have occurred to him at all but for the prompting of a grand and dignified, beautiful and human old nun.

Perhaps life would have continued on in this way: comprised of comings and goings across the ocean, the Channel, the Alps and the plains; returning always to the place which was, for us, as earth is to all flying things, the center of gravity and everything.

But our dreams and desires, important as they seem to us, are not much after all when put up against an undefinable entity sometimes called vaguely "world events." When war came, it cast its shadow over all of us, sparing least of all the village of Senlis and all the other villages of Europe which had no hand in bringing on chaos but were far less equipped to escape it than the criminals who had. And when France was finally threatened, there was nothing for my father to do but send his family back to America.

He and George stayed on for many months after we were gone, winding up affairs which as far as business was concerned were extremely small, but in matters of friendships and conscience were great. There was no doubt that my father was greatly troubled over the idea of leaving France just when she needed all the loyalty and help of those who loved her most. To flee seemed hardly the proper payment of gratitude for the unlimited goodness she had bestowed upon him. And so all the while he helped others to acquire passports and make preparations to leave, he thought over the matter, trying, I am sure, to keep the memory of the Ohio wild country from bearing too heavily upon his choice in the matter.

In the end, it was Monsieur Gillet, the Curator of the Abbaye de Challis, a learned and kindly man who had been his great friend for many years, who helped him to convince himself that there was little he could do but follow his family.

"To remain," said Gillet with a French practicality which defied all romance and nonsense, "would be a heroic gesture. But Frenchmen already know of their plight, although I doubt if many Americans do. Perhaps it would be better for us if you would go and tell them."

So at last my father packed up his furniture, determined not to leave one of those fine old eighteenth-century works of Norman woodcarvers for the Boche to haul away, and prepared himself to leave the Presbytère forever. As he went about his packing, he scattered little tokens of his guilt and sadness about him. All the royalties he earned in France were left in the hands of those who could turn them over to the French underground when the inevitable moment of its birth arrived. All the toys we had owned he distributed with an air of apology among the little boys of Senlis, who so often had caused him to shake with amusement as he watched them dragging their long loaves of French bread, wrapped in the middle and bare at both ends, through the dusty streets of the village at dusk.

He offered Louise, the martyred cook of all those Sunday lunches, a place in America at a largely increased salary, a proposal to which she replied with a hearty laugh, "Ah, merci, Monsieur, but I could never be happy there. This is my place." And I believe her certainty only increased my father's sense of guilt, and perhaps his envy. For how simple it seemed for Louise, with her solidity, her spirit, her peasant's love of work, which was indeed the breath and life of France, to know her place.

And then, a few days before they went away, Senlis gave George and my father a tribute and a farewell that would lift their spirits, warm their hearts and give them hope for France, whenever they thought of her even in her most terrible moment. They had been sitting on the terrace one morning in the bright autumn sunshine having some of Louise's special pancakes for breakfast when suddenly they were deluged with water from a cloudless sky.

Leaping to their feet, shouting, "Sale vache, merde alors, what in the name of Christ goes on here?," they caught the sound of a proudly emotional "Marseillaise," and looking in the direction from which the sound had come, they saw on the bridge that spanned La Nonnette a wonderful scene. There, all around a shining new motor-drawn fire engine, the first in the history of the village, stood the Senlis fire brigade in the delightful process of carrying out a special demonstration for Monsieur Bromfield et Le Hookans.

As they watched, the hose was lowered into the canal, motors roared and a new flood assailed them—Urrou, whoosh,

> *Allons, enfants de la patrie,*
> *Le jour de gloire est arrivé!*
> *Contre nous de la tyrannie,*

drip, drip, drip, splat. . . . And then a sweeping bow from Monsieur Duvalier, the fire chief, as his heroic voice boomed above the roar of the pump and the hiss of flying spray.

"Bonjour, messieurs, voilà, c'est arrivé. . . Ah, ce monde moderne est vraiment magnifique, n'est-ce pas, Monsieur Hookans?"

Perhaps it was desire that made it so, but often afterward my father told of the odd sensation he had gained from the hilarious racket, the grand bow and the proud voice that boomed cheerfully across the waters. "It was almost," he said, "as if the brigade had come that morning to assure me. 'Don't be alarmed,' they seemed to say, 'they cannot really defeat us for they don't know how to laugh as we do. When you come back, we shall still be here.'"

In the end, they said good-by to them all: Louise, La Mère Supérieure and her little nuns, the fire chief, who had drowned their pancakes and given them courage, Messrs. Gillet and Piquet.

Piquet, wrapped in his stomach flannel, with his pack of jolly stories in his head, went off to war and was never heard from again. And that spring the phlox and chrysanthemums grew thin and spindly and died in the faded light of the chapel without ever truly being warmed by the sun.

5

The Return

"Then I pushed open the door and walked into the smell of cattle and horses and hay and silage and I knew that I had come home and that never again would I be long separated from that smell because it meant security and stability and because in the end, after years of excitement and wandering and adventure, it had reclaimed me. It was in the blood and could not be denied. But all of that story I told long ago in The Farm.*"*   *L.B.*

How often it has been said that all the things we love when we are children are kept in our memories much larger and finer than life until we see them again when we are older and, supposedly, wiser. On that day, after a second look at their disheartening unremarkability, we are supposed to bid farewell to all our last childish illusions.

If this is the case, then my father's good fortune was all the greater. For he had known the Ohio country as a boy who had fished in its streams and roamed its forests with a child's unflagging hope for adventure and it had all remained very grand in his memory. Yet, when he returned with a hesitant and suspicious heart, he found it all more richly and excitingly beautiful than he had dared imagine it to be during his absence. He had not been deceived. Instead, he had found his youth there, waiting and intact. And something more as well, for he was able to greet it and look upon it with the perception and vision of an older man.

He named his place Malabar Farm after the Malabar Coast of India because that name bore many beautiful connotations he wanted always to keep in mind and because it was with his earnings from the Indian books that he was able to buy the land. It was not what a banker or a real-estate agent or even a cold, purely practical farmer (something very difficult to be) would have considered a sound investment. Its soil had been worn thin by years of bad, unimaginative farming. Deep gullies slashed its hills and remained like open wounds kept festering by wind and rain and never allowed to heal. Its pastures were slowly giving way to cocklebur, Scotch thistle, poverty grass and creeping blackberry brambles: the final stage of land which has been abused by foolish, thoughtless men who have no business calling themselves farmers, keepers of the precious land.

But from the low, broad valley across which a little stream, called Switzer's Creek, cut its shallow, wood-shaded swath, the green Ohio hills—the first foothills of the Blue Ridge Mountains —rose wondrously on every side. Here the hills were covered by aged forests of oak, maple, elm, sycamore and ash, left mercifully and wisely by the Scotch and English and German farmers who had walked in over the mountains a hundred years ago; who had understood and left to their children an understanding and love of trees. Elsewhere, they rose beyond the gnarled, wind-tormented trees of an old orchard to end sharply in cliffs of pink and yellow sandstone over which the wild grape and trumpet vines extended their coarse, woody ropes and dark greenery as if to conceal remnants of some near-forgotten, savage past.

There was a maple-sugar bush, which when my father saw it again for the first time in many years was gray and leafless and laden with snow. But seeing it thus, with its old shed where the boiling vats lay rusting under the snow, turned over for the last time by hands that knew well the incomparable fragrance they produced, he must have thought of how it all would be in spring when the sap coursed toward pale leaves and smoke rose again from the battered chimney.

Above the sugar bush, and the taller trees which stood over the maples like strong, protecting brothers, was a high, windy and deeply grassed land which, in spite of many attempts, had never quite been tamed by the hands of man. From the top of its great, tree-bald dome, one gained an illusory view of the Ohio country, in which houses, roads and all signs of modern civilization were eclipsed in the vast sweep of forests and lakes and gray-blue distances. Looking over it all, one was brought back to the chilling and reviving sensation of man's solitude in the beginning of things.

Altogether, this was the kind of farm which Pa would have bought and struggled gallantly and hopelessly to restore. It had suffered many a dull-witted, thoughtless owner, but it had always been meant for a big-hearted, imaginative man who was something of a dreamer and could see in every bend and hollow and proud hill the answer to some special yearning.

My father was just forty when he returned to Ohio and, but for increased knowledge gained over the years, perhaps the best way to express the difference in him is to say that he hadn't changed so very much, but simply ripened. For although we may improve our manners, increase our savoir-faire, become more tolerant in some ways and less in others, it is doubtful if any of us ever really succeed in overcoming the basic traits, good or bad, that make us. If at some time we actually come to pretend or even to believe that we have overcome them, we simply deceive others, and worse still ourselves.

As it was, the Boss never made much attempt, if any, at basic change, and so at forty he was more of a stubborn, willful, mood-ridden, raging tyrant than ever. Even though he deplored his own weaknesses, he defied others to consider or criticize them.

This nervous state of being resulted in scenes at which the innocent bystander was *dared* to show signs of surprise, shock or any other form of disapproval. "If you don't like it, you know what you can do," his eyes warned as he called us "idiots, gland types, psychopaths, gold brickers," and accused us of everything from outright deceit to calculated homicide and subversion by persecution. Under fire we screamed right back so that the dreadful noise must have been truly terrifying to that "innocent bystander," who might as likely as not have been an amiable Fuller Brush man, snatched up on an impulse and invited in for lunch.

But no less astounding was the manner in which two or three minutes after the most dreadful row, we were all laughing and talking gaily again as if all our days passed in Louisa May Alcott–like cheerful and unbroken composure. The results of this strange behavior were twofold. For one thing, in later years with our own families we never bothered much, either, with controlling our tempers. For another, hanging on to our sense of humor, we were always able to forgive the Boss any outrage as long as it was ridiculous enough to give us a good laugh later on.

I will gladly admit that there were other reasons as well for his earning our forgiveness. For even when he raged, there was a certain lionlike fascination about him of which he, too, must have been fully aware. The thought of this amused and softened us. For it made us aware more than ever of the fact that our father was in every way intensely human. As well as the tyrant, he could be, in the space of a day, delightful and amusing, sage and assuring, uninhibitedly generous and incredibly tender at the most unexpected moments.

The Fuller Brush man must have sensed this as well. Else why, with all his illusions about the great man shattered, should

71

he have come back again and again? (We were not, after all, very good customers for his brushes.)

These were my father's traits, little changed since the day he'd had a violent row with Ma and gone off to join the French Army. Physically he was tall and angular still, and leathery from countless days spent in wind, rain and sun from Jahore and Sumatra to the cold, brooding winter countries of Scandinavia. At the corners of his eyes, the crow's-feet, made from laughter and looking into the sun, mingled with other lines of weariness and dissipation, which gave him the look of a man who had lived a great deal, both by day and by night. He had fished and swum and walked along country roads and, at the end of the day, relished perhaps more than his share of good food and drink and satisfying talk. He had hungered for and devoured music and literature, observed the thoughts and behavior of all kinds of people, both brilliant and dull. He had tasted nearly everything worth tasting in life, and the impressions of all were stamped in his humorous, canny blue eyes, while the dissatisfied hunger for more showed in his outthrust, perpetually determined jaw.

When he came home again, America struck him in the same way that she strikes most Americans who have lived for a long time amidst the changelessness and solidity of the old world. He found his country to be almost frighteningly dynamic, its people rootless and nearly hysterically obsessed with success and change. The more it seemed to him that Americans were unstable, constantly in motion and striving for "the good life" through dependence on one another (generally termed cooperation), the more his entire being yearned for the stability and independence of the old life he had left behind somewhere in the Ohio country and which he was determined to rediscover. Because of this anxious determination, sometimes in the beginning at Malabar Farm he would sit in the evening on the porch with one friend or another whom he had not seen in many years and there would begin a conversation something like this:

"You must hardly recognize the America you left behind," the friend would say with obvious pride and enthusiasm, "so much has happened, everyone is so prosperous and well fed. It looks as though the American dream has paid off. It would be hard to find anyone today who can't seek and achieve 'the good life.' "

My father would nod in agreement, but already there would be a quizzical look in his eyes.

"No, I suppose there are only a few left behind—mostly poor white trash, driven out of the dust bowl," and he would stare threateningly at his friend. "Don't for a minute overlook them.

"Still, I'll tell you something. I find this American dream business pretty damned frightening at times."

"Now just what do you mean by that?" the friend would counter, already anticipating the superior sour-grapes attitude of one who had long been an expatriate. "Isn't that what you howled so about in your first books and articles, putting an end to the exploitation of the many to enrich the few, so to speak?"

"Of course I did," the Boss would snap back. "I lived in the midst of it as a boy. I used to make the rounds as a reporter right in the town of Mansfield. I saw plenty of squalid flats, six people to a bed and sleeping in shifts at that. You don't need to give *me* a moral lecture on the worth of collective bargaining. That isn't what worries me. It's the instability that comes with great industrial cities, the mess it puts people's lives into, the way a man loses his roots and ties."

"Oh, come now, you're talking about security?" The friend would be ready with a fool-proof formula for modern security, but he was never allowed, unless he was Frank Lausche or someone else equally impossible to intimidate, to give voice to it. For my father would lean forward, piercing his friend's self-confidence with an accusing stare. "You're damn right, that's it. Good God, if you think for a moment that iceboxes and a new car every year on the installment plan, or even old age benefits are security, you're out of your mind! That's just the trouble," he would go on, by now thoroughly excited by his subject. "We're all too dependent on one another nowadays; even the farmer who instead of raising his own food grows cotton right up to the door. All we need is a crisis for the farmer to have to find some way to eat his goddamn cotton because nobody'll be able to buy it and he's lost his credit at the canned-goods store."

"If you're thinking of a depression," the friend would lean back in his chair with the confident air of one who *has* lived close to the scene, "that could never happen again. The government's got to keep things running smoothly these days or . . ."

"Christ!" The bellow of a wild bull would cause the alarmed friend's drink to fly up and splatter over an already well-marinated porch floor. "It makes my hair stand on end to hear that crap about government control. It's just because of that that we're all such self-satisfied goddamn lazy fools!"

As suddenly as he exploded, he would become quiet again, and, looking out over the lower pastures which the last of the day now covered with a soft, golden light, he would say, "I came away from Europe because it was being destroyed by dishonesty and rottenness and greed and there was nothing I could do about it. I came home to find the security I've often dreamed about, which seemed to me perhaps existed only in America. But I haven't found it. I think it has been destroyed by people like you, who think that subsidies and old age pensions can be put in its place. If I'm ever to have that security," he would add quietly, "I can see that I'll have to make it myself; a world of my own that's solid, complete and apart. That, by the way, is what I'm going to do, right here on this farm, or kill myself trying."

74

The defiance and certainty in his voice, as he uttered this ultimatum, were such that the friend would either bow his head in pity at the writer's romantic naïveté, or regard him with a new sense of wonder that could never again be quite destroyed.

In either case, there was nothing on earth that friend could have said that would have made my father pause for a moment in his determination to make Malabar Farm all that he had often dreamed it would be.

6

The Farm and the Plan

We came to Malabar Farm in early spring, which is an important condition in the matter of fixing a farm in the heart. We saw the winter whiteness that covered the hills and burdened the limbs of trees dissolve, under the cold misery of March rains, into thick, sucking mud which dragged off our boots a hundred times between the house and the barn. The mud and rain, chill and sorry, converged upon Switzer's Creek, swelling it to the proportions of a roaring river. It lapped at the groaning iron frame of the bridge, grating its underside with bits of driftwood and trunks of fallen trees which, once the rains had ceased, would lodge to form deep pools where trout streaked temptingly silver in the summer sunlight.

Then, as the sun appeared, its light glancing off the plows in the field and warming the plowman's chilled and sodden bones, we became aware, suddenly, of the smell of an Ohio spring. It was a combination of thawing manure in a clogged barnyard (a smell that is not unsweet), of earth opening and grass breaking through and, as one bent searchingly toward the ground, the miraculous scent of violets to convince one that the earth dared not freeze again. The warmth that had touched the earth, entered the roots of trees and made the sap stir and rise until it reached the outermost twigs and there produced the first childlike greenness, telling us that it was time, at last, to begin our farming.

It was a rudimentary job the first year, of getting as much into the ground as possible with the materials at hand: a John Deere tractor, plow and disk and a pair of handsome gray Percheron mares. Farming is like that, especially in the beginning. While you dream and long for it, spring comes without warning and you are caught between rains, running helter-skelter, doing the best you can.

But all of us were taken with a wild enthusiasm for the farm, even Nanny with her inherent English love of roses and good vegetables in the damp earth, and George, who acted as kibitzer, making great fun of our labors and photographing Nanny in compromising positions as she bent over her seed beds. Together we managed, along with the planting of corn and wheat and potatoes, to root willows in the banks of Switzer's Creek to bind the earth against next spring's torrents and to plant roses and lilacs about the big, ugly house into which we had moved, in the hope that its crudeness would soon be softened by their growth.

The ewes, bought with the farm, were ancient and dropped many orphans that had to be fed cow's milk from Coca-Cola bottles and raised with the goats which already more than sufficiently occupied our porch swing.

The goats were incredibly destructive: eating the bark from young saplings, making holes in the roof of the Ford station wagon, so that it was necessary, when it rained, to drive under the shelter of an umbrella. They even devoured manuscripts, and when their destructiveness became too chaotic, my father would regard us all with a look of stern resignation and murmur, "I'm afraid we'll just have to take them up to the Ferguson Place."

Our corresponding shouts of delight were not born of childish insensibility to the banishment of our pets, but of the well-founded belief that there was not a fence on that high, lonely outpost of the farm that could contain the little beasts anyway, and that their removal to the Ferguson Place was simply a poor excuse during a busy season for a walk in the woods.

With the dogs, sheep and goats at our heels, we made a strangely Zenobia White, Annie Spragg–like procession as we headed in early afternoon toward the woods, where the sunlight pierced the shelter of the trees and touched the earth below with warm patches of light. We ran crazily from one patch to another, our feet rustling through the winter's old leaves, spreading them apart to find masses of yellow and purple violets and white trillium clustered like fallen stars among the roots of great trees.

The road we followed was impassable to cars. Sheltered by the trees, its earth was always damp and cold, even in the drought of August, and in many places it was worn away to a bare shelf of sandstone and shale over which spring water trickled from somewhere deep in the earth. Walking along this road in the shade of the tall trees, one had the sensation of having come unexpectedly upon a part of a great, enclosed world which had avoided, or perhaps even defied, progress. It seemed almost as if the noise and clatter and brassiness of the modern age were prohibited here and, knowing this, one felt extremely grateful. At the top of that road, we passed through a sagging gate and came upon the great dome of wind-swept grass that was the Ferguson Place, high above the Ohio country.

There was an orchard of peach trees, the fruit of which was small and touched with the concentrated sweetness of fruit gone wild with time. And near by, a pair of tall spruce trees creaked and groaned in the wind over the front steps—all that was left—of a house that had been razed to the ground long ago. No one knew how the house was burned but it stood as another proof that civilization had been tried on the Ferguson Place and, like an illness, cast off.

It was as impossible to drag heavy machinery up that weather-beaten road as it was to drive a car, and so my father made the Ferguson Place into an immense pasture for the herds of beef cattle. With time, as they roamed over the land, the cattle trampled out much of the thorn and berry bush and seeded white and red clover with their manure so that the earth flourished and grazing became lush and plentiful.

The cattle grew fat and dropped healthy calves and thrived in their lonely life above the trees. And whenever we human beings climbed the hill to look them over or find a little peace of our own on the Ferguson Place, they all came running to greet us as if they had had their fill of solitude and would like to "get shed" of it for a long while.

Sometimes we'd come in the evening to collect fallen branches and trees which had died of age or been broken by wind or lightning. As the light faded from the sky, we would build an immense bonfire and settle down to eat steak and roast corn, drink boiled coffee, sing songs and tell stories as the fire roared upward and sent its sparks toward the star-lit hood of the sky. Then the cattle would gather all around us in a circle and stare entranced, their white and roan and black faces oddly illuminated in the dancing light of the fire.

That was as near as the Ferguson Place ever came to being "civilized" in the present sense of the word, and that was quite near enough. No swarms of cars full of curiosity seekers, no one who would have sought that hidden place simply out of a desire not to miss anything ever got to the top of the hill. For only those who loved a long walk in the wood for no other reason than to smell the forest smell, know its lights and shades and coolnesses and the solitude beyond, could go there any time they chose—on foot. Only they, at any rate, would have understood it.

For all of us at Malabar it was a private place where one could sort out one's own troubles or, if we were filled with some special joy, shout it to the wind up there, with only the grasses and trees and wild creatures startled in a fence row to share our abandon. All of us respected the sanctity of its seclusion and no one ever accompanied anyone else up that steep, forested trail without first being invited.

Undoubtedly, the world's tormented souls would be in far better shape if every man had a Ferguson Place to go to or, at least, if every man understood the full value of such private beauty and solitude.

Certainly this was so in the case of my father. The only emotions he ever really cared to show were those of rage and amusement. The rest he kept for the Ferguson Place. He could not have become neurotic, for he was too strong, too healthily explosive, but it would have been infinitely more difficult for him to live and to think things out had it not been for that lovely, untamable land above the trees.

On those goat-exiling days, we were noisy and exuberant and full of adventure. We covered most of the Ferguson Place, climbing to its crest and then down the other side to sit on the houseless steps for a time, smelling the fragrance of old spruce needles and young lilac flowers and speculating on the memories of the log cabin which had been the Fergusons' dwelling before the house had been built, and which was sinking now under the weight of storms and wild honeysuckle back to the rich earth from which it had arisen. In fifty years—soon in time, distant in a lifetime—there would be nothing left but the lilac and the spruce if only (and that was our silent hope) progress could continue indefinitely to be defied.

When we had rested a little, we returned home by devious trails. My father had by then forgotten our existence and wandered off on his own, leaving us to find our way as best we could.

More often than not, his head full of new ideas aroused by his walk through the woods, he would not turn home without first stopping at the house of Max Drake, which stood sheltered by an immense aged elm tree on the other side of Switzer's Creek.

Max was the farm manager, a darkly handsome young man, who had the strong, square hands, good humor and soft, unruffled speech that one finds among those who have been raised in the country with a great love and understanding of all that is country living.

Among those who were, as he put it, "too old and 'sot' in their ways, or . . . too young and too eager, too innocent of the hard work that is inevitably a part of farming," the Boss had been looking for Max for a long time. When at last he found him, he wrote of him: "He was himself the son of a good farmer. . . . He was interested in anchoring the soil and salvaging what remained of our good land. And he was interested also in the whole intangible side of a farmer's life which had to do with farm institutes and square-dancing and fun."

These, evidently, were what my father considered the necessary prerequisites for a good farm manager, and he was right. In finding Max he made an excellent choice, probably the best in his lifetime. For not only was Max all these things; he was intelligent and curious and had a mind and will of his own.

I think Max became, as most people did, deeply attached to the Boss from the start. Certainly he had enough vision to respect and admire in my father an even wider vision which could perceive magnificent horizons and encourage others to see them and (though he often failed himself) gain them. Yet Max was never overimpressed. He was aware as well that such an imagination was likely to lift a man like my father to such heights that he might never again regain the not quite so bright reality from which he had risen, to see things as they were. Thus, while Max's wife, Marion, a handsome, auburn-haired young woman with a shy, hospitable country manner, served them beer and sandwiches, Max sat down with an enthusiastic but occasionally dubious look on his face as together he and my father went over the plan of the farm.

Thomas Wolfe is right, of course. You can't go home again.

For in the space of a lifetime people and places and situations change so drastically that the "old life" loses its place in the whirling confusion of new inventions and growing populations, new conceptions of living and the politics to fit them. Yet that was what my father tried to do in the beginning at Malabar Farm. In many ways, he failed, for it was no longer possible in this day of interdependence to return fully to the old life in which a man's world is entirely his own. That era, except for a few remote regions of the world, is finished. My father had declared so himself over twenty years ago, in *The Farm*. But of course in pushing constantly into the future we need not break all ties with the past; and even though in many ways it was a failure, the first plan of Malabar Farm served as a basis for another kind of richness to come, to be recognized and shared by a great many people, giving them a new vision and lease on life.

The plan was roughly that of a co-operative farm, on which each family would earn a good salary, have a house rent free and all the necessities except those staples that could not be grown on the farm. In order to provide these necessities, it was to be a general farm, with beef and dairy cattle, hogs and chickens, a large common vegetable garden and fruits in season: grapes, currants, gooseberries, peaches, plums and tart apples, and, of course, the maple-sugar bush restored to working order to sweeten our country meals. My father was to finance the whole thing until a profit was made, and then, after taking the first 5 per cent for himself, the profit was to be divided among the families who lived and worked on the farm.

Sometimes, perhaps because even then—though I understood little of what they talked about—the atmosphere of beer and pickles, cigarette smoke and farmers talking about the land somehow fascinated me, my father used to take me along on the return through the wood, from the Ferguson Place to the Drakes' house. Then I would sit back in one of Max and Marion's comfortably shabby armchairs and listen as they went over the plan.

When the Boss discussed contour plowing, the planting of legumes to restore and enrich the soil, or allowing the forest which had been grazed down by sheep and cattle to grow back thick and lush once more, Max would lean forward, at times almost falling out of his chair with an eagerness and enthusiasm he could not contain. But then the conversation would turn to the subject of feeding ourselves almost entirely from the farm and suddenly Max would lean back again almost as a passenger seated in a car next to a reckless driver automatically leans back and puts his foot out to brake the disaster he knows it is not within his power to avoid.

"Somehow, I just can't believe in it," he would say in his soft, unargumentative voice, "not with the cost of machinery and labor what it is today. Why, more than half those things you can buy cheaper than you can raise them yourself."

This comment, placed so calmly, as an unalterable fact, before my father, caused the usual noisy reaction. "Good Christ, that's just what I've been trying to get across ever since I got back to this country," and then he would begin all over again about the sad plight of the farmer who grew cotton up to the door and ate canned vegetables in midsummer.

Still, when the speech was over, Max would retaliate in his quiet way, wondrously unperturbed, it seemed, by the uproar. "I see your point; see it very well. But I guess we have to live with it, Mr. B., or go broke trying to match a factory hand's wages. That's why my dad sold his hogs and chickens and stayed with just the dairy. Things got too complicated. Couldn't even find a good hand and couldn't do it all himself. Get into too many things here and we'll have the same kettle of fish. Nobody wants to work on the farm any more."

But the Boss was never one to agree he had lost an argument —especially one in which his heart was so set on the rightness of what he had said; and seeing that his adversary was not going to "scare easy" he would try a new tactic. Regarding his farm manager with a fatherly look of pity, he would begin again.

"I really can't blame you, I suppose, for these damned half-baked ideas. Where'd you go? Ohio State? Not that it makes any difference. But just listen to me for a minute, and remember, I am twice your age and I've seen quite a lot—a hell of a lot more in fact than any of your autocratic college professors quoting from revised editions of that goddamn bible, *Morrison's Feeds and Feeding,* year after year. What they know about economics you can put in a U.S.D.A. pamphlet and chuck it into the wastebasket.

"Now listen to me. You never saw the kind of farm I'm talking about because they did away with it here before your time. But it still exists in places like France and Belgium, a progressive, thrifty island of security, not of the kind that buys an icebox every year. That's phony. But of the kind where a man can dig himself in, in times of disaster, live well, feed himself and his family and even his friends. Do you see what I mean?"

Max, seeing the trend of conversation moving in a direction beyond his reach, would grow quizzical.

"I'm afraid I don't know much about France and Belgium, sir. But if you'll excuse my saying so, it seems to me that I've heard from you yourself that Europe's growing old and kind of stagnant. Our country is young and dynamic—do you think you can fairly compare the two?"

"Stagnant!" Remembering with a sudden upsetting clarity a dissertation he'd brought forth the night before about Europe's creeping senility, the Boss would seem to feel a certain sense of stagnation himself. But as rapidly as he had fallen into Max's well-set trap, he pulled himself out by rejecting the argument from the contradictory point of view and beginning afresh on the ills of progress in America.

"You're right. We're a rich country, I won't deny it, the richest country in the world, and we got that way by taking what the farmers started for us and building a great industrial economy on top of it. But now, for the love of Christ, our 'standard of living' is pushed down our throats morning, noon and night. We feel as though we must work, live, buy and buy more to maintain it. The fear of losing it has made us into a lot of gullible nincompoops."

He would glower for a moment at Max and then seemingly soften again with pity. "You can't know, Max, how can any young American who has to fight against this incredible swamp of propaganda know that there are other things besides a standard of living, such as roots, and land passed on from generation to generation. You've heard of the wines of Alsace and Burgundy? How do they do it from century to century?

"No, wait a minute, they're not toiling slaves as you picture them, but small prosperous farmers who send their sons to universities and to know the world."

Max would remain silent for a moment after the Boss had spoken, caught at last in the shrewdly descriptive web. He'd never thought of it that way before, of having the standard of living forced down his throat, but perhaps it was true. He'd had an answer for every one of those arguments about "cotton up to the door," but now indeed where were they? Undoubtedly, it would have helped a great deal if he could have gone off on an extensive tour of the vineyards of Burgundy before giving his response. But his one feeble pawn, the recollection of what the Boss had said the night before about Europe's growing stagnant, had gotten lost somewhere in a rich, tantalizing glow of often irrelevant but strangely convincing words. To find the thread it would have been necessary to think all night. So, laughingly, Max would, without surrendering, put an end to the argument by saying, "All right, sir, you've got me by the tail. I disagree about this business of general farming and

85

self-sufficiency. I don't think it will work. But I guess the only way is to give it a try."

This said, the two would turn toward the plan again, in their faces youth and eager, sleepless excitement, not unlike that of a revolutionary's, defiant against the world. And soon they would be engrossed in the more pressing details of remodeling broken-down barns, restoring eroded fields and bramble-strewn, grass-bare hills and earning themselves a bit of money.

As they talked, the moon rose to edge the thin spring clouds with silver, and in my armchair I fell asleep unnoticed and forgotten, often until the small hours of dawn.

7

The Big House

"There is a kind of aura about every house I have ever entered, so strong that I believe I could tell you a great deal about the owners after ten minutes spent within the walls—whether the wife was dominant, whether the family was happy or unhappy, and almost exactly the degree of education and culture and knowledge of the person who built and furnished and lived in it."   L. B.

How true were those words written by my father when applied to his own house on the hill overlooking the lower pastures of Malabar Farm. If the Presbytère was a reflection of his character, the Big House was even more so. For the walls of the Presbytère echoed still with soft footsteps of ancient monks, but although an old Ohio country way of living was blended into the building of the Big House, still the laying of every floorboard and the raising of every wall originated in the heart and head of its owner.

Only a man smitten with an irrepressible love of theatrics and grandeur could have built in the living room of a farmhouse a mirrored wall, spangled at the top with forty-eight gilt stars and a golden American eagle, or installed an old pink marble fireplace from some long-past great house in New Orleans, or covered the grand, sweeping double stairway with deep red plush carpeting.

This accomplished, my father, with a fanatic hatred of the protective fussiness of middle-class housewives, proceeded to trudge up those stairs daily with boots thoroughly muddied from tramping in the fields. Before that enormous gilt-spangled mirror in the living room he laid a carpet with a bright enough design in it to disguise the spots made by countless generations of puddling puppies. And because variety is the essence of life, he adorned that elegant and beautiful marble mantelpiece with a sculpture of his favorite dog, created with mystical dexterity out of clay by his daughter Anne, a handsome bust of Lafayette, a pig's embryo preserved in plastic and a clod of Malabar's most fertile topsoil.

He conceived of a house with many rooms for many different people and made them spacious and cheerful enough to suit everyone's longing for lightheartedness and warmth and a noisily rambunctious and yet inexplicably peaceful existence. The old chairs from the Presbytère, still covered in their faded Brittany cloth, came to rest within walls lined with books and gay paper patterned in a design of strawberries and cool, green leaves. The guest rooms were large and airy, and the sunlight filtered through clean muslin curtains. The little lavatory beside the front door had a gilt mirror, gold and red velvet curtains out of *Nana* and a photograph of a fat and bonneted garrulous American mother-in-law declaring in large print, just beneath her pouting bosom, "Rest room, hell; I ain't tired. Where's the can?"

One could seek and find laughter any time one wanted in the Big House, or peace, or solitude, or good company. And one's rage or grief was given vent and quickly lost in the atmosphere of a house big enough and diverse enough to allow each of its inhabitants to live as he pleased.

The Big House grew as an immense addition to the simple, kindly, two-story frame house that my father had bought with the part of the farm called the Herring Place and which looked across the lower pasture and Switzer's Creek to the "mail-order house" where we were encamped.

Unlike the "mail-order house," which my father described in *Pleasant Valley* as having been built without knowledge or taste or regard for beauty, but simply to show off the success of its owners, there was nothing pretentious about the house of Clem Herring, from its big roseate-and-yellow sandstone kitchen in the cellar, to the sitting room and parlor for deaths, births and marriages on the first floor.

The twin doors of those rooms opened onto a simple stoop from which Clem and his wife had watched the setting sun fill the valley with a pale bronze light for perhaps fifty summers or more. They had tended their land as best they could, but in the end they had to give it up because of a common tragedy which often occurs to people who love the land. Their children had not inherited their love and there was no one, now that they were old and feeble, to look after things. The farming strain, as it so often does in America, had quickly run out.

The Herring house, like so many in Ohio, gave one, on seeing it, a yearning to live as one might have lived as a child, amidst old, worn and indestructible things, sheltered by the trees and untroubled by the world. And, oddly enough, in spite of its new scope and grandeur, when my father added on the Big House, room by room, level by level, he managed to maintain this sense of quiet and continuity with an old and dignified country past. He did it with wooden porticos and cast-iron pillars in designs of grapes and leaves from old houses along the Ohio River; with here a fanlight from a house in the original Mormon settlement of Kirtland, and there dormer windows copied from an old inn at Zoar. He did it by adding one wing after another, slowly and thoughtfully, as if, indeed, he had in his mind taken on the form of different persons in different generations, beginning simply and expanding the house as the farm had grown and prospered. The final effect was such, when all was completed, that it was difficult to remember, even for those who lived there, which had come first: the old orchard behind, the great white barn below, the broad-leafed catalpa and giant black walnut trees on the lawn, or the house itself, so comfortably shaded, so at ease in its setting that it might have been there for centuries.

There were plenty of places in that house, once we had moved into it, where my father could have gone to read over and answer the countless letters he received every day. He tried them all, one by one. But for some strange reason, in the end, he came to spread his correspondence over the dining-room table and work there for most of the morning every day.

The door from the pantry to the dining room never stopped swinging with the passage of children and dogs and people on flying errands. With every fresh entry the papers on the table flew up and scattered in great white drifts while my father glared at the door and struggled hopelessly with coffee cups and ash trays to secure order. And yet, although this must have occurred a hundred times every morning, he doggedly insisted on holding his ground.

The dining room in early morning was especially delightful, for the sun shining through its large bay windows seemed to bring the garden and the farm right into the house. Through the front window, one could look out over the lawn and watch beyond the black walnut tree the boys with the wagons and tractors passing by on the road below in the healthy, busy activity of a farm's green season. Through the back window, one saw the orchard and calf pasture, full of ornery long-legged heifers and bull calves, kicking their heels and sending up sparks of dew in the morning freshness; or a chipmunk frozen on the fence, caught in the act of stealing last year's berries from a bank covered with white multiflora roses.

Within, the sunlight shone on walls of baroque Austrian

green which might have been too violent but for the softening effect made by the lovely faded colors of old French prints of fruits and flowers, the white borderings of woodwork and the sparkling crystal chandelier—an immense and intricate work which hung over the center of the table and gave the room, which was otherwise simple and countrified, the air of being always ready for a gala affair.

The buffet which had supported the burden of so many Sunday lunches at the Presbytère sagged cheerfully, like a handsome old woman whose fine features can only be enhanced by the ravages of age, against one bright green wall. The sight of it always managed to renew in my father his satisfaction at having succeeded in rescuing his beloved French furniture from destruction by the Germans.

The furniture stood now, safe forever, in this beautiful house he had created all by himself. And so, sitting in the dining room in early morning, struggling with wind and mail and all, he could look out the great bay window over the farm, glance about him and think to himself, "Everything is here that I have ever really wanted," and, so saying, come very near the truth.

We watched the Big House grow and came in the very beginning to love it with the eager love of children who have scampered over a house's foundations and played hide and seek among its roofless walls as gradually they rose toward the open sky. Then, one day, the big front door, set in its handsome white portico, with the potbellied figure of Ganesha, the Indian God of Plenty, in a niche above, stood ready to be opened.

My father grasped the handle and pushed it open. And, as Nanny stood by clutching her hair and agonizingly shrieking, "Ooh, ooh, ooh, oh, damn the ruddy mutts," seven boxer dogs leapt into the hall and, slobbering and panting, sped on muddy feet from one room to the next before they returned at last to welcome us in.

The Heritage

There it was, finished at last, shining and new, smelling still of fresh-sawed wood, paint and wax, yet already strangely homely with the old things: the Valois chaise longue and rotund Norman bureaus, like old friends turned up unexpectedly to blunt the shock of one's over-new surroundings.

That was on the first day, in the spring of 1940. Before very long, all the rooms were filled with people who had come for a weekend or forever. And by the time autumn came, the polished floors were worn dull in familiar paths, and the chintz-covered sofas were pleasantly faded. Lafayette on the mantel had become accustomed, it seemed, to sharing his laurels with the pig's embryo, the clod of earth and Voltaire, who sat— as in France—among his books on the other side of the room.

From the little balcony off the nursery, Nanny's petunias hung in purple and lavender frills like the indiscriminate flounces of an old lady's petticoat. Wisteria had clambered over the iron pillars of grapes and leaves and invaded the portico, where sparrows had set up housekeeping protected by Ganesha's numerous outstretched arms. And already to everyone it seemed as though the Bromfields had lived in the Big House at Malabar always.

8

The World of Aunt Julia Post and Mary Wood Bromfield

We had not long been living in the Big House when one fine autumn day, clear and crisp and wondrously suitable to the occasion, a chauffeur-driven black limousine appeared on the driveway before the house. It came to a halt just at the foot of the lawn and from it stepped a tiny old lady who, dropping a garter and ignoring it with great dignity, crossed the lawn toward my father, who came hurrying with outstretched hands to greet her.

"Why, Louis," she cried in a voice as clear as the ring of true procelain, "I never dreamed you had such a vivid imagination. It's all really quite lovely."

My father took this double-edged compliment with the grin of a pleased boy and, while the chauffeur with elegant discretion got rid of the garter amidst the luggage, he escorted our Great Aunt Julia into the house.

In a little while, having disposed of her luggage with a wave of her hand, she was seated straight and commanding in a big, comfortable overstuffed chair in the living room, surrounded and being waited upon by all of us. In her presence, my mother seemed at once radiant and slightly ill at ease like a pupil in dread of erring before an old and excellent teacher. My father, used to being the dominant, spectacular center of everything, seemed oddly awestruck.

I can't say exactly what it was about this woman no bigger than a child that commanded such respect in us all. Perhaps it was her very delicacy and smallness that made it possible for her to dominate a roomful of people. Her entire being, pale-skinned and blue-veined, seemed as fragile and brittle as fine china. And yet, looking at her, one somehow felt that that delicate exterior contained within it a fire of will and strength greater than any of those about her. One saw it in her blue eyes, which, surrounded by a mass of wrinkles made by both laughter and sternness, were clear and piercing. One sensed it in the sound of her voice, which, without ever being raised, was listened to attentively as one listens thirstily for the sound of spring water deep in the rocks of a forest ravine.

Some faces become flaccid and pulpy with age or sunken and hollow, as the strength of youthful flesh slowly deteriorates along with the character that was not very powerful even in youth. But where the character is strong, as in the case of my great aunt, the aged, wrinkling skin only seems to heighten the effect of the fine vigor and beauty of structure beneath it. Aunt Julia's cheek bones and nose were sharpened with age, her deep-set eyes made deeper still, so that one saw, almost as if the skin were but a veil, the ultimate fineness of years of good breeding: a fineness from which the next generation, without new blood, might reap a harvest of decay.

But for the moment, in this little woman, it was perfection which kept us all watching, breathlessly, as if a great actress had appeared to act her part upon the stage.

She chatted with us, leaving no one out and touching all, yet never with banality, so that one felt upon being spoken to that an answer was expected, waited for and sharply weighed, and when we had all been talking long enough, she turned abruptly to my father and said, "I hope lunch will be soon.

This autumn air makes me ravenous. And when lunch is finished, while Mary has her rest, I want you to take me over the farm. I want to see as much as I can before dark. Do you realize I've never been West before?"

After Great Aunt Julia's stay at Malabar, which wore down even my inexhaustible father, I went with Nanny to visit the old lady every time we took a trip to New York. And while she and Nanny conversed politely, Nanny discreetly "keeping her station" amidst almost lordly grandeur and Aunt Julia tactfully bowing to Nanny's whim, my eyes roamed in unending fascination over the rooms which contained so much of the world from which Aunt Julia and my mother had come.

It was an antique world of perfect taste and convention preserved for such a long time that, although one admired immediately its delicacy and beauty, in a little while one was taken aback by a sensation of depressing inertia.

Indeed, little had changed in the routine of Aunt Julia's life since she herself had been a child. Her summers had been spent in Ipswich, Mass. (as my mother called it with the familiarity of one who leaves the pronouncement of Massachusetts to outsiders), amidst green lawns shaded by ancient elms and quiet ponds whose calm waters were broken only by the drifting of haughty white swans. Her winters were spent in New York in that spacious, old-fashioned brownstone house where, amidst its collection of spare and beautiful old relics, she dictated the lives of her kin. There she entertained members of her family (like them or not) on Tuesdays and Fridays at dinner. On other days she admitted various members of, or candidates for, the Social Register into her presence. She had made the grand tour as a girl and again as a mother with her daughter, Harriet, whose resultant first husband had been a Hungarian count.

It was an elegant and fascinating world, shabby with the disdainful shabbiness of those who have long lived and believed in Puritan austerity and the "solid coin." And living within it must have been a great deal like existing as a museum piece under glass which might crumble into dust on contact with fresh air. Its laboriously constructed walls of convention were that vulnerable.

Such was the world in which my mother existed until my father unlocked the glass cabinet and exposed her to the air. To him, an eager, charming, slightly raw young man from the Midwest, it must have been infinitely fascinating for its very loftiness and dignity, like some distant inaccessible star. What did this dignity mean? What did this distant world contain of which it was so proud?

He soon discovered that, like all worlds, it was not, after all, so inaccessible and, once he had attained it, that the mysteries it contained were not exactly of the sort he had expected. He found that indeed, boyish and scantily educated as he was, he understood far more about the harshness and glories of the world than these highly refined and literate people. They were like an exhibit of past values to which the present, stirring, progressing, free breathing, had no relation.

Who cared any longer, in truth, about the Appleton-Wood-Post family tree? Or whether a Wood made a proper marriage, preserving a fine old Ipswich tradition? Where was Ipswich, Mass., anyway? Only the Appletons, Woods and Posts knew or cared and only my father among a few, by marrying into the family, discovered the quiet, sunlit, doomed charm which lay about those green lawns, cultivated roses and shaded ponds. It delighted, intrigued and horrified him, and when he had become thoroughly enough immersed in the sensations of this world, he wrote a novel about it, one of his best, called *Early Autumn*. In it, he described the trivial uselessness of such a world and the manner in which its distorted values affected the lives of people with hearts and souls and human wants who existed within it. Abandon, splendor, barbarism and passion were not permitted to enter; and yet they all slipped in under the door and, hidden in the guise of piety, often found release only through cruelty, morbidity and madness. Some were content with it. For others, there was no release at all except through total escape. In the story, some did escape, while others were able by their strength, intelligence and sense of duty to live within and above it.

In reality as well, there were some who took themselves out of the museum cabinet world. My Aunt Harriet was one of them: a tall, handsome, vigorous and arresting woman who came to live in the great world and face it with a strength and brilliance which always enabled her to conquer whatever situation confronted her. Others were shattered by their contact with a hard and wholesome air, went a little mad and became cultists, meditators and Buchmanites.

Among those who escaped was my mother. She neither quite managed to master the violent world which confronted her, nor was she ever entirely conquered by it. Always, it seemed, she lived just between, at times appalled and terrified by what she faced, at times bursting forth with a tremendous courage and presence of mind which seemed to come from some hidden reserve she hardly knew or was ever allowed to know she possessed.

My mother escaped, and I am sure at the time of their marriage my father felt that it was he who had performed the rescue. All his life he had a way of becoming entangled in the lives of others, making up a story about them, arranging what was best "to suit the story" if not the victims themselves, until they became totally incapable of disentanglement. It was better for some, worse for others.

It is hard for me to be sure whether or not my mother would have been better off left within her old, fragile, pampered surroundings. I think not. For although she was totally unprepared to face the bold, challenging life of the Boss, I think her very intelligence and sense of humor would have had to reject the world from which she had come. In life with my father she found something exciting, fine and romantic to the very end.

And yet, to the end, in many ways my mother was an extremely lonely woman. For my father, with his great energy and ambition, a struggle was part of the pleasure of his life and defeat was unthinkable. But my mother never enjoyed a fight for its own sake, was at once repelled by the idea, and immediately sought peace and defeat.

My father, in spite of his need to be surrounded by people, was all the same a strangely solitary man who needed, just as much, a moment to be alone with his thoughts. He cherished privacy, and when he was performing a rescue it never occurred to him that afterward the one rescued might be dependent upon him forever. It seemed only natural to him that my mother should make her life just as he made his, drawing strength and comfort from her own resources.

But in marrying him my mother had totally conceded her life to him to do with as he pleased. When she discovered that he intended to do nothing, then the long, growing loneliness began. She was not strong enough, not capable really of making her own life. She needed rather to confide and to be protected and receive affection as proof of the necessity of her existence.

My father may have needed affection (it would be a cold, barren world if any of us didn't) but he didn't live for it. And, probably because a nature as dynamic as his always dominates everything around it, his children as well shared his horror of showing affection. If any of these feelings ever came spontaneously to the surface, they came in response to a love for Nanny: a simple mother-child affection which comes with sleepless nights, work and sacrifice, scolding and shouting and the remorseful embrace. My mother in her glass cabinet world had never been taught to make these things a part of her life. And in her strange apathy, which was an illness worse than the illness of her heart, she conceded them all to Nanny; just as, one by one, she delegated to others she considered more strong and capable all the duties of a mother and mistress of a household until there was nothing left to do.

In France, the emptiness in her life was not so apparent for there were the countless trips to India, Italy, Switzerland, England; the round of gay evenings in Paris; the Sunday lunches at the Presbytère, over which she presided as hostess. In this role, she moved from person to person, group to group, laughing and talking in her open, friendly manner, with a certain charming naïveté that made all feel at home and at ease.

But in Ohio, although there were countless trips, they were always to bond rallies or Farm Bureau meetings which scarcely bore the glamour of the Continent. And although the house was generally full of people, they seemed to roam at will, independent of a hostess's supervision or entertainment.

How lost she must have felt in our midst. For what was there in that busy, purposeful Ohio life that others could not do better than she? And where was there that others went that she could follow? Her weak heart forbade her to climb the high hills. For her there was no Ferguson's Place, no touch with the land and life that absorbed the rest of us so thoroughly from dawn to darkness.

"At least," she used to cry pathetically, with a defiant little laugh, "no one can say I am not a good hostess!"

The trouble in that energetic, vital life of ours was that no one seemed to think they needed a hostess. We were all so busy, so able, so energetic and such confident fools as to believe that nothing more was necessary.

How sad for us that we so often are unable to see, when it is there, a grace and warmth that exists all about us because of the presence of a single person. It was there in the room my father built for her next to his own, which had once been the parlor for the Herrings' deaths, births and marriages. It was filled with all the old things from France: the bulging, friendly Louis XV bureau, the ivories on the mantel. The light shone through the ruffled curtains in the same way that it had in the Presbytère, somehow different from the way it shone in all the other rooms, so that here again was that inexplicable peace.

One felt it the moment one came into the room. Somehow, shouting halted at the door and a peculiarly amiable reasoning took place within, albeit a defeatist reasoning which laughingly begged, "If it gives him pleasure, if it means peace, then let him have his way." So, as in France, a great many crises ended in amused gossip and never reached my father. And one left the room with a strange, unaccountable sense of well-being, which remained as the memory of autumn sunshine remains long into the winter.

It was odd that such a calm could emanate from someone whose nerves were at times so tormented that her trembling hands could scarcely hold a book or a pair of knitting needles or a glass of sherry before lunch. And yet, that calm was what we hurried toward in the morning, carrying the breakfast tray, our heads full of laughter and gossip.

Still, by afternoon our attitude had changed. As she roamed the house from one busy room to another, always hoping wistfully but not knowing how to become a part of our constant activity, we threw up our hands in worldly impatience at her helplessness.

And who set the pattern of our senseless cruelty but the Boss himself? He would not tolerate any rudeness or lack of respect on the part of any of us and many were the times that I suffered the experience of being "flattened out" as he put it, for being caught making fun of my mother. But how was I to resist when in the next moment I would hear him shout in mock torment, "The water, Mary, is it boiling? For Christ's sake, you mean to say you can't tell?"

Almost inevitably, George would follow up with some such

taunt as, "Look at Mary, the Martyr, boiling an egg with such stoic forbearance."

Sometimes she would laugh, amused in spite of herself. Sometimes she *did* bear it silently, like a martyr. Sometimes she simply wept. But never could she succeed in overcoming the helplessness which had been a part of her teaching since the days when she was a child.

When we had been living at Malabar for several years, my father wrote a novel, *Mrs. Parkington,* of which, although she never came from the West or married such a fabulously human and wicked character as Major Augustus Parkington, my Great Aunt Julia Post was indisputably the star.

Susie Parkington, like Great Aunt Julia Post, seemed to live countless lives, each one vivid and full of experience, while those around her seemed to live only one life, and that trivial, short and pointless. With her own great strength and self-containment, she sustained the tragedies and disasters of her family, solving the troubles that none of them had the character to solve for themselves. With each experience, her knowledge and love of life deepened and strengthened, so that as an old woman she was always capable of dominating those around her with her spirit, will and canny intelligence.

Aunt Julia Post was the Susie Parkington of the novel, and the weak, unbalanced "Blair strain," who believed still that membership in Harvard Clubs provided a carte blanche for weakness, stupidity and dishonesty, arose like a pitiful shadow out of the world from which Aunt Julia and my mother came.

Often, during those years when Aunt Julia came "west" to Malabar, I saw people watch with delight my father and the old lady at the game of matching wits. They might begin by screeching at one another about the farm. "The fields are so green this year, Louis dear. What's that you put on them?"

"Manure, Aunt Julia. Wouldn't do any good in Ipswich."

"Ipswich, my dear boy, was sustaining a growing population

with or without manure before Ohio was even heard of." They'd go on to reminisce about Lillian Russell, Lichine, Caruso, in the end inviting one another to meet in Rome for a performance of *Traviata* in the spring and then sadly recalling that Rome was at war and New York and the Metropolitan would have to do. By the time our great aunt's holiday in the West was over, the two would have scheduled a meeting for every day that my father was in New York for the next year. That my father would keep them all there was little doubt, for in all the world of actors, painters, writers, grandes dames, White Russians, diplomats, Social Register numbers and Bowery bums who were his intimates the moment he set foot in New York, no one gave him more pleasure in an evening of matching wit for wit, touché for touché and laugh for laugh than this delicate and incredibly enjoyable nineteenth-century lady who was my mother's aunt.

How different things might have been if my mother could have possessed a little of the fire of that old lady who had emerged from the same world as she. She possessed all her aunt's charm, grace, humor and discernment, and yet a single ingredient was missing: the power to make a world of her own and from it confront the world around her. In the end, it had little to do with the ability to boil an egg. For I am sure the old lady was as incapable of that as her niece. It was some other quality, which said, "Look here, I am what I am and defy you to make me dependent on anyone." It was that which would have so quickly satisfied my father.

With the years, my mother's understanding and tenderness deepened. She became more and more tolerant and there was greater peace than ever to be found in her quiet, sunlit room. But the peace was touched with sadness. For young and pretty as she looked, her hands grew old and trembled and her eyes came more and more to hold a distant, abstracted look, as if she were waiting for a moment that was yet to arrive. Somehow in her heart she never seemed to stop hoping that one day my father might come home across the fields and, with a protective smile, accept the gift of dependence she had offered him when, long ago, he had rescued her from the glass cabinet world of Aunt Julia Post.

9

Home Life

Malabar Farm is the farm for me,
A place of unbridled activity.
A farm is always in some kind of tizzy,
But Bromfield's farm is really *busy:*
Strangers arriving by every train,
Bromfield terracing against the rain,
Catamounts crying, mowers mowing,
Guest rooms full to overflowing,
Boxers in every room of the house,
Cows being milked to Brahms and Strauss,
Kids arriving by van or pung,
Bromfield up to his eyes in dung,
Sailors, trumpeters, mystics, actors,
All of them wanting to drive the tractors,
All of them eager to husk the corn,
Some of them sipping their drinks till morn . . . *

From the sound of the Strauss ballet drifting through the widely flung French doors and the sometimes hilarious, sometimes querulous babble of voices on the evening air, it might have been the end of a gay, rowdy Sunday at the Presbytère. Only now the chairs were set out under the catalpa trees, where

* From "Malabar Farm," a book review by E. B. White. Reprinted by permission of E. B. White; Copyright © 1948 The New Yorker Magazine, Inc.

a flock of guinea fowl perched, mingling their ear-splitting squawks with the conversation, and the drinks which at Senlis had made gay patterns on the flagstone terrace now nestled patiently in the grass waiting to be rummaged for. Old faces from other times mingled with the new. There was Clifton Webb, blinking rapidly and self-pityingly over a huge mound of onions, and Ina Claire with tomato juice dripping from her elbows, and Joe Munroe, who had come over, innocently enough, to take pictures for the *Farm Quarterly;* and perhaps a gaunt, pale-gray East Indian who had appeared, as if by rope trick in reverse, out of nowhere to discuss the possibilities of asceticism in a Western civilization. Unreceptive to the idea of sitting cross-legged and unbathed for days at a time staring into space, my father had refused to discuss the matter but left the Indian in the front hall, where he had sat, for days in a row, contemplating his bare feet, until this moment when he found himself with all the others, immersed in a jungle of vegetables from which there seemed no earthly escape but that of chopping one's way out.

In the center of the circle, my father sat before a huge tub, washing tomatoes with a hose and making sure that no one was left unsupplied and without work. The moment someone paused, heaved a sigh and fumbled for his drink in the grass, the Boss would rise, heap a tray full of vegetables and, with an admonitory "Them that works, eats," dump the load in his victim's lap before returning hastily to his sadistic scrubbing.

The activity was an old one known to all thrifty farmers as "getting set for winter." In this case, the concoction was a mysterious compound of tomatoes, carrots, onions, parsley, celery and countless herbs to be boiled, bottled up and drunk in the snowy season as what Nanny called, with a note of irony in her voice, "Dr. Bromfield's Tonic."

The setting on any other farm might have seemed somewhat extraordinary; but at Malabar, glorified tomato juice (because that was what it added up to) was inevitably prepared on the lawn under the evening stars to the accompaniment of frogs croaking in the swamp, guinea fowl squawking in the trees, music drifting through the open door onto the agitated twilight air.

If it wasn't tomato juice, it was something else. It was, for instance, not unusual to find Kay Francis disguised in a Greta Garbo get-up, complete with high-collared greatcoat, dark glasses and cigarette holder, stirring apple butter in a caldron at arm's length with a wooden hoe. This Endor-like performance, also on the front lawn, attracted—even way out in the country— more excited spectators than summer carnival.

I have, in my time, seen Joan Fontaine hurry out in her negligee and slippers to witness the birth of a calf; and Lady Patricia Ward at the bend of the road, waving a willow wand, and crying with a hysterical little tremor in her voice, "Stop, stop—oh, I say, this is a bit too much," to a herd of stampeding cattle.

All of this was the result of my father's new mode of entertainment, based on the axiom that guests should either be useful or stay out of the way. Oddly enough, in spite of the "chores" for which most were—to put it lightly—inadequately equipped, the system seemed to work. Proof enough was that never, in all my years at Malabar, can I remember one of the ten bedrooms not being fully occupied and often sofas in the living room and hammocks on the porch as well.

Occasionally rebellion occurred against this modern form of (them that works eats) human bondage. I chuckle all over again, though many years have passed between, when I visualize the appearance of Mayo, Humphrey Bogart's third wife, after spending an entire afternoon crawling through barbed-wire fences in dogged pursuit of the Boss on one of his marathon cross-country treks.

As she stumbled over the threshold of the living room, her mink coat in shreds, looking more than anything like Clark just arriving from the Northwest Passage, Bogie, who had wisely taken my father's latter offer of "keeping out of the way," looked up from the easy chair, where he reclined in a smoking jacket and slippers, and greeted her with an amused, "Why, Mayo dear, you look a bit effete this evening."

In answer, one of my mother's favorite Venetian lamps went whizzing past Bogie's left ear, and in an instant the entire room exploded into a cyclone of books, ashtrays, whiskey bottles and all imaginable items that could be lifted, swung and hurled.

My father, the true cause of this dramatic outburst, emerged unharmed and howling with delight once the battle (there being nothing left to throw) had come to its conclusion. On another occasion, however, punishment was dealt with greater justice. Columnist Inez Robb, just back from the harrowing experience of covering the African Campaign, had come for a quiet rest in the country. Unfortunately, her "rest" had coincided with the greatest overproduction of tomatoes in the history of Malabar's vegetable garden.

Morning, afternoon and night, everyone had been chopping and boiling and looking up with the harassed expression of a lot of distressed Helen Hokinson housewives as the gardener hauled in one loaded bushel basket after another.

At last, on the evening of the fourth day, which was Sunday, the Boss summarily ordered the stove cleared to make way for the weekly ritual of preparing Sunday-night supper. Magically, every sign of the red-splattered turmoil was dispersed and, in no time, every pot and pan, knife and cutting board was enlisted in the business of making scalloped oysters, Spanish omelet, onion soup and an enormous salad of everything that had missed being sacrificed to Dr. Bromfield's Tonic.

Being acquainted with Mrs. Robb's highly strung nature, one might have expected her to toss up her knife at the thought of cooking something else and stalk off to bed for that long-coveted "rest." But knowing Mrs. Robb and my father collectively, it was easy to realize that such behavior would have had the exact same effect as raising a white flag of defeat. The two, rival columnists in nearly all the same newspapers, and chronic prima donnas on all occasions, never rested a moment in one another's company. It was rather like putting Callas and Tebaldi on the same stage, and in view of this it was quite natural that Mrs. Robb, instead of going off to bed, should go to work on some rival cookery of her own.

My father was so immersed in the occupation of rolling cracker crumbs and daubing butter that, but for an occasional "For the love of Christ, where are those onions?" to a weeping drudge at his elbow, he scarcely noticed anything going around him; much less Mrs. Robb's secretive stirrings on the corner of the stove. It was only when all were seated around the big table, complimenting his exotic dishes with appropriate gluttonous noises, that he discovered to his great consternation that his rival had caught him off his guard.

Suddenly through the swinging door burst Mrs. Robb, holding a large steaming bowl provocatively high in the air. "Nothing like good *plain* Iowa cooking," she crowed, bustling with a dreadful domestic smugness around the table. "Do try some succotash. It may help to settle your stomach," she added, casting a calculatingly negative eye over my father's indigestible assortment of delicacies.

Immediately the air became tense with expectation. It was as if someone had thrust a sword into my father's hand. Wrinkling his nostrils distastefully and drawing as far away from the apparently odious dish as possible, he gave a horrified moan, "Revolting! Christ! How *can* you abominate two perfectly delicious vegetables by mixing them together and then have the nerve to call it plain cooking? I bet anything you put cornstarch in cherry pie, too." He fixed Mrs. Robb with a hard, accusative stare. "You do, don't you?"

Mrs. Robb's response was quick, effective and remindful of

the fact that she had just recently returned from the war front. With a flick of her thin, supple wrists, she squarely dumped the entire contents of the bowl over my father's head.

For an instance, corn, beans and butter cascading about his ears and eyes and over his shoulders, my father sat notably stunned, incredulous and quiet. Not so my grandmother, however, who, in defense of her children, had had some fifty years of practice in snarling like a wounded lioness. From her chair at the end of the table where my father had carefully placed her out of hearing, she now leaped to her feet with the agility of a ten-year-old and, wielding her cane, bellowed in Wagnerian tones, "Hessian! Treating him thus and sharing his room and board!"

In the next moment all seven dogs rose in unison from beneath the table and pounced on the spilled vegetables as if they'd been starved for weeks. The table rose in the air. Salt and pepper shakers flew ceilingward, the scalloped oysters were immersed in a sea of beer and Ma's cane, rather than descend upon the object of her original fury, was put to the task of flailing away at a swirling mass of ravenous boxers.

It was a terrible battle, which only ended when the Boss, tearing apart Prince and Rex, the two main opponents, tossed one through the open bay window and the other through the swinging door to the pantry. For a moment, in the utter silence that followed, he slumped into his chair, panting and triumphant from the fight. He sat stoic and immovable, his hair stiff, his face yellow and cracking in places.

For quite a while, no one made a sound and then there escaped from Mrs. Robb the most delightedly vindictive giggle. In response, my father's shoulders began to shake and the butter on his face disintegrated into thousands of weird crevices. Soon everyone was laughing loud and noisily; everyone except Ma, who sat staring glumly at the wreckage of her hero's food and board.

From that day on, Ma never spoke to that "Hessian" again, but Mrs. Robb bore her cross with great forbearance. She returned again and again to match my father's wit in politics, history, philosophy, cards and plain nonsense, even during tomato season.

Obviously, there had to be other rewards for the long trip to Malabar than obstacle courses across the fields and drudgery on the lawn and in the kitchen. It must have been a blessed change for most of those who came to the farm from the constant busyness of great cities to wake in the morning and have breakfast in bed while the sunlight filtered through the feathery leaves and branches of the walnut tree into those large, comfortable, cheerful rooms.

It must have been good to eat the plain, delicious country cooking—chicken and peas and mashed potatoes and corn-on-the-cob all dripping with butter, all far too good to spoil with a fancy sauce; the tart pies of apples or grapes or blackberries in season. My father used to lean back in his chair and chuckle derisively while actresses and society dames stowed it away like a lot of ravenous fieldhands.

There were, as well, long evenings of music and talk and laughter, interspersed with entertainment often provided by the guests themselves. It might have been a performance of *Firebird* in the front hall by a traveling ballet troupe on its way West, or Larry Adler, piercing the lovely stillness of a starlit country night with the clear, melancholy notes from his harmonica.

Then, too, any evening during the spring and summer, it was quite possible to stumble into a Farm Bureau meeting, with an assembly of funeral chairs in the living room and the forty pieces of the Lucas High School Band in the hall. For the hall and the living room were built to accommodate all these things: Farm Bureau meetings and brass bands and Larry Adler alike, or even a relatively quiet evening by the fire.

In the end, I have a feeling that all this was because my father

The dock from which Ellen learned to swim in the pond in front of the Big House at Malabar.

View of Malabar Farm from the sandstone cliffs behind the Big House at Malabar.

Louis Bromfield by the pond used to irrigate the vegetable garden.

The view down the valley from the Big House.

The big barn and Anne's studio at Malabar.

A human ant spreading manure across a cornfield at Malabar.

Winter view of the Big
House at Malabar.

Anne Bromfield, 1940.

Ellen and Louis Bromfield inspecting corn at
Malabar Farm, around 1938.

Hope, Ellen, and Mary Bromfield with the spaniel Dusky and the boxer Prince
outside the "mail-order house" at Malabar.

George Hawkins and Louis Bromfield with the boxers Rex and Prince and the golden retriever Rory.

Louis and Mary Bromfield at Malabar Farm.

Lauren Bacall and Humphrey Bogart were married at Malabar Farm, May 21, 1945.

Talking to the Sunday visitors on the top of Mt. Jeez.

had long ago concocted the story of his life. In it, he saw himself as a wise and generous man who had experienced the world and knew how to live. His table was laden with good food and drink and his house filled with good books, music, intelligent and lively people. All were welcome who were possessed of wit, kindness, sincerity and a desire to live. Only the humorless, the pretentious and the self-righteous were not allowed to get through the door a second time.

Generally, in the Big House, the theme of my father's story carried through extremely well. When it didn't, when we showed signs of sinking into the most sinful station of all, "dullness," my father merely disappeared to the hay fields, leaving us to fend for ourselves in the midst of our mediocrity while he mowed. Sometimes he mowed until dark, leaving staggering amounts of hay behind to be frantically windrowed and gathered by the farm hands, before an approaching thunderstorm that threatened to ruin half the summer harvest.

Quite often, alone and at peace in the open fields, the idea would occur to him that it would be wondrously refreshing to have some of that good talk about crops and politics that he and his father had often found on their long excursions through the country just before elections. Once the idea had "taken hold" there was apparently nothing for it but to hurry home as if driven by a brush fire and get George on the phone to invite all the neighbors in Pleasant Valley for a farm party the following evening.

At the proper hour—seven o'clock—the dining-room table was covered with cakes and sandwiches for the Shracks, the Oakes, the Mengerts, Zodys and Cullers who would arrive soon after chore time.

The first time they came, they sat on the edge of the old Valois furniture, self-conscious and not a little suspicious, stiff as Grant Wood's proud, wooden plains people until George passed the punch, personally spiked to stir boldness in the most hesitant breast. Then these upright figures began to unbend, lined faces crinkled into warm, outlandish smiles, as gradually they remembered how Charlie Bromfield and his son Louis used to roam the countryside at election time, sometimes stopping for an evening meal or to spend the night in the loft above the stable. And, watching my father's own smile in a face every bit as sun-creased and burned as their own, they began to discern that he had not changed much after all, in spite of his "fancy living," and that, further, he had invited them that evening because he hoped that they would still find him to be one of them.

Toward eleven o'clock, for there were chores to be done at dawn, they would don their tweed coats and leather jackets and depart, scattering heart-warming fragments of approval which could be heard through the door when they were only just on the other side.

"A lot like the old man—got the same smile." "Full of queer ideas, but by the looks of his hands he's a dirt farmer."

"Ain't high and mighty like I expected."

"The Mrs. seems downright nice. I *wonder*, do you s'pose she'd think it funny being asked to come to a sewing circle?"

The next time they came, Grant Wood wouldn't have found a subject among them. Punch was accepted at the door, the folks sat back in the French furniture, and crop talk and politics flowed as freely as a cocked barrel of cider at apple-picking time.

Indeed, if my father had wished to return to anyone, it was to these people: the men who had long cared for the crops and the women who had tended the herds and looked after the chickens and put up fruits in season, their faces creased now with diligence, now with laughter as they bent over their bottles and kettles. They would not have changed their hard, busy lives and the pride it provided them for any of the soft attractions of easy city living. They were his kind at this moment, and they, too, were part of the story of the wanderer coming home to discover that his values were much the same as they had always been, only strengthened now by long years of roaming.

It was to these people and to this land that my grandparents had now returned as well, after years of never quite feeling at home anywhere else in the world. They had come to live in a bright, sunlit room with a balcony from which Ma could peer endlessly over the petunias and watch with her insatiable curiosity and love of activity the busy world of the farm.

Pa, tall and thin, still erect, still with the look of a ghost in his eyes, had returned to roam the valley he had loved and struggled all alone to save from the ravages of a seedy civilization long ago.

He had not been so happy in many years and, before long, we discovered a strange thing about him. As he wandered each day from farm to farm, neighbor to neighbor, he never lost his way. Stepping briskly through the front door and falling over the steps, the existence of which he'd forgotten since the day before, he would announce that he thought he'd take a walk up the road for a chat with old man Gwynn. And there, when evening came, we'd find him seated on the broken-down stoop of Gwynn's silvery gray house, stroking the ears of an immense old-fashioned collie and talking about trotting horses, what to do about this year's mortgage and how sweet the berries were on the hill where the poverty grass was too thin to graze even a few cows any longer.

He had come home, it seemed, to live totally in the past. He had forgotten none of his old friends' names, and if their faces had changed and weathered considerably with the years, perhaps it was part of his ability to go back in time to imagine that they had not; and not to notice if, here and there, a son had replaced a father who had already gone to his grave.

In all that valley among the elms and oaks and sycamores which, aged like himself, had changed little since his departure, nothing was unfamiliar to him except the house in which he lived. There he recognized no one but his wife and son and, confused by all the unfamiliar faces about him, he wandered again like a polite phantom. He read the same newspaper day after day and looked with constant expectancy to see if his daughter, Marie, who had died six years earlier of pneumonia, would not, among all these strange people, walk suddenly into the room.

But once he stepped out in the morning air and set off on one of his jaunts, his pathetic state left him. He was erect and sure and happy again. Looking back now and remembering the sight of him seated on the stoop with his old friend Gwynn, it seems to me that of the many who have set out in their hearts to return to their beginnings perhaps my grandfather, who could remember nothing at all but a distant past, had succeeded best of all.

Ma was little changed. Her yellow-gray wisps of hair may have been thinner, but she still set them in tightly regimented waves about her square, bulldog's head. She still galloped at a fair pace, swinging at the dogs with a cane, and could never find enough to do.

In those last years, for a time it seemed that a kind of truce arose between my father and this strong, sentimental old woman whom he professed to be his avowed tormentor. It was not that he ceased to call her a cheat at cards, or to place her at the foot of the table, where she glowered at him, gnawing her ears of corn like a lioness wishing for something a bit more substantial. No. He kept right on teasing her and never letting her have her way. But there were certain things about the farm which Ma understood better than anyone else, even himself. For more than her husband and son, whose romanticism often got the best of their practicality, Ma was a real farmer. She knew with certainty where the best apple pies and tart pickles and cream and butter came from, what made them perfect and what didn't. She could pick out instinctively with her sharp, searching eyes the good cattle from the bad and tell what had caused a field of wheat to grow thin, or to rust or lodge.

And so, every day toward evening, when things cooled off and the mellow light was not too strong for an old lady's eyes, the two would set off together in the jeep for a tour of inspection. They might go off up to the Ferguson place to judge how the steer were fattening on the grass or to crush the new-mown alfalfa and brome grass hay between their fingers and smell the richness or the poorness therein. It seemed that in those moments at least he longingly and humbly sought the old woman's approval and that, to her, must have been akin to a reward from the angels.

Pa died first, going almost apologetically, with as little fuss and stir as he had lived. Ma died a year or two afterward. She had a heart disease which fought incessantly to quell her, but I don't think it was her heart that got the best of her in the end. I think it was the fact that there was no one left to look after.

On the day she died, she first did her laundry in the bathtub (she refused ever to let any "slatternly washerwoman" touch her clothing) and finished all the family mending. And then, in the night, as if suddenly realizing, horrified, that there was nothing left to do, she gasped her last breath and went.

She had, with her sentimentality and love of ceremony, long planned to be buried beneath a monument with a long, flowery tribute inscribed on it in the family plot in Mansfield. But even in death my father refused to let her have her way and, declaring the Mansfield cemetery vulgar and barbaric, he buried her ashes with those of Pa and his sister, Marie, in the tiny cemetery on the hill at Malabar.

It was indeed a beautiful place, with roses on the fence and the simple, primitive stones of the first settlers who came to the valley, all overgrown with myrtle and honeysuckle. The stones of Ma and Pa and Marie lie side by side and on Ma's stone is a simple verse:

The Heritage

She was a Force, nature itself
Incarnate, now smiling, now distraught,
Powerful at once and gentle as a
Breeze, Ceres and Cybele and
Juno all in one and like the
Elements, forever right. L. B.

It is a beautiful verse and appropriate. And yet I can't help thinking that a still more truthful script might have been added: "Here lies Annette Coulter Bromfield, much against her will." And I can't help wondering, either, exactly what it was within my father which would not allow him to give in to Ma, not even in her death.

Everything Ma possessed was dispensed over the household to continue life in a merry and useful way. I remember with tears of laughter in my eyes the sight of Mrs. Byerly, the laundress, falling in a faint at the bottom of the stairs as George appeared at the top, a swarthy replica of my grandmother, clothed in her black alpaca coat with its warm caracul fur collar, leaning on her cane, his mustaches peeping grotesquely from beneath Ma's old black hat with the red cherries on the brim.

A few weeks later, Ma and Pa's room was occupied by a young French count with hay fever and a fine sense of humor who wanted to learn about farming, and that was as it should have been. Those rooms were made to live in the present, remembering happy days and carrying on life with all its goodness and laughter. Heaven forbid that in such a household as my father's any room should ever have become only a suffocating memorial to the past.

 # 10

The Lesson

Wherever I am, whatever I am doing, I have only to stop a moment and listen to recall the exact sound of water pouring into my father's boots as he walked down the middle of Switzer's Creek. There was a kind of muffled roaring as if a couple of miniature dams had burst and then a delicious gurgling as the waters poured in over the boot brims.

He would half smile to himself with a look of wonderful contentment which seemed to say, "So much for that, now I am free!" and then, soggily, he would forge ahead to meet the pleasures of the forest and stream with the unlimited enthusiasm of a happy, cautionless child.

In his eagerness, he waded always twenty or thirty paces ahead of everyone else. But his perception was as sharp as his zeal, so that he seldom missed anything worth seeing in spite of his exhausting pace. If a deer flicked softly as a phantom among the patches of sun and shadow in the forest, or a tall gray crane stalked sedately out of the stream ahead, he was inevitably the first to catch a sight of it. Coming to an abrupt halt and putting back his hand for silence, he would murmur only, "Look!" his tyrannical voice suddenly soft with awe as he watched the great bird rise from a standstill in ponderous, beautiful flight.

Sitting looking at an inkwell on my table, I can feel again the cool, deep shade of the forest and the sudden, welcome warmth and radiance where the sun shone through a break in the forest roof left by a fallen tree. I can hear distinctly the constant rippling of water over pebbles and around rocks and the sudden, silent flow where a deep pool had been hollowed out of the river bank by the floods of last spring. Sometimes, when we came to such a pool, we stopped a moment to sit on the sandy bank or lie along the smooth, outstretched limb of a birch tree to watch bass and sunfish hovering and darting in the calm, deep waters below.

I can smell again the mucky, rich odor of the swamp where the land dipped away from the banks of the stream and amidst the decaying roots of trees the slimy black earth sprouted marsh marigolds, which glowed in the eerie light. Often, with slow sucking noise, we pulled up plants and wrapped them in my father's water-soaked shirt to carry home and plant on the edge of the spring pond at the bottom of the hill. There was always something in my father's shirt before the walk had progressed very far: black forest earth to put around the begonias in the dining-room window; the first gray, spongy morels of spring, excitedly gathered from among winter's dead leaves; a struggling, wounded coon to be tended and later set free.

Holding his precious cargo aloft, he would plunge into the stream again and wade on until he came at last to the swimming hole, a place where the steady, rippling flow of Switzer's Creek had been broken by the fall of a great elm tree.

On one bank of the stream the fallen tree was secured by the tangle of its roots, intricate and massive enough to play a game of tag in. On the other bank, its great, slowly dying crown was held firmly by a boulder of sandstone, left by the glaciers, perhaps at the very time when Switzer's Creek first came into existence. Tumbling over the tree trunk and around the aged moss-covered rock, the stream had hollowed out a deep pool which all summer long was clear and cold where the feeble sunlight, shining through the trees, never quite penetrated its depths.

The moment he came upon the swimming hole, my father would lay his bundle of slimy marigolds or the still mildly protesting raccoon in the shelter of the rock and, stripping down to his underwear, dive off the log into the pool.

We followed rapidly, one after another: dogs and children plunging wildly in every direction so that the pool, a moment ago silent but for the deep, hollow sound of its little fall of water, exploded suddenly with glistening spray and the sound of shouting as if we, too, had exploded after the silence of our long walk.

When we had splashed enough and shouted enough to suit our childish exuberance, we threw ourselves exhausted and cold on a little beach of white sand and rounded pebbles built up by the swirling waters of the pool. The beach lay just beneath the open space in the forest roof that had once been covered with the branches and leaves of the now fallen tree. The sun shone pleasantly through the gap, drying us and warming us as we rested and watched snapping turtles appear, cautiously out of nowhere, to sun on the now safely deserted log. And when we had tired of this, we turned over on our backs and lay, sometimes for hours, looking up at the intricate pattern of leaves and branches close to the sky until it seemed as though, with a kind of floating headiness, we had become part of the pattern ourselves.

Yogi and all the other nonsense that has to do with mysticism never found a better device for losing contact with the petty problems of humanity. It is neither necessary to stand on one's head, nor to deny oneself a bath or seek a God who exists above and beyond this world. One has simply to come clean from the river, lie in the warm sand, look up at the trees and find heaven all about. It is a trick I have often since used to lift myself out of intolerable depression, one that I learned from my father when he taught us our first lessons about living on the farm.

They were not the kind of lessons one might have expected— the kind my grandmother would first have taught about where the apple pie came from and how to keep the ledgers balanced with the renderings of the dairy and the field. Those were important lessons, I'll admit, and commendable, too. But they would have had little value if we had not known those other things as well; the ones we learned by such time-wasting occupations as walking down the middle of Switzer's Creek.

But my father, busy as he was, always had time to look for a fox's lair hidden in a crevice behind a curtain of cold-flowing spring water; or stop to watch a quail beating her "broken" wing, sending up a spray of morning dew to lead us away from her nest in the field.

Nor was it only the sight of these things that he brought to our attention by his crying, "Look!" "Sshh, listen!" he would whisper, and made us aware of the sounds and, in our silent attention, the smell of so many things that one would never have thought of as having either a sound or a smell.

He taught us to know sound and smell of morning, when everything is still fresh and glistening before the wind and dust and heat of the day give the earth a tired look. At just about dawn, the mourning dove gives a cry so gentle and melancholy that it would never be heard during the constant roaring of the day. It is a cry that belongs to morning and freshness, just as the shriek of the screech owl belongs to the awesome stillness before dawn.

The very quiet is a sound. Then add to it the sawing of the crickets, the throaty swallowings of a bullfrog, the sounds of water. We listened for the minute, exclamatory jumping of a fish, the silent ripple of a muskrat across the pond in the moonlight, the muffled ring of steel on stone, as a horse stumbled down into the stream. And in the night, "Sshh, listen!" a tap and then another. Was it really? And in answer, a steady pounding which said, "All is well, go to sleep now, for the rain is coming and the roof is over our heads."

And so, because of our father's "Looks!" and "Listens!" it was possible for us to make, with our imaginings, the farm the domain of our private fantasy. The autumn fields and shadowed, leafy places along the stream, the stars above a blazing fire on a lonely hill on a summer night were all ours: our winds, our shadows, our stars, our fantastic and beautiful world.

Once you have known the land in such a way it is of little importance whether or not you have your property in the limited legal sense. Somehow, somewhere in your heart, it is yours forever and you will do everything to care for and protect it as long as any power to do so remains. And even when there is no power left, you will never forget, you will always compare and search for that feeling again. And so that is why I say it was a powerful and good lesson that my father taught us in the beginning. After that, he need never have troubled himself about our concern with the farm.

Out of those first years at Malabar Farm came a book called *Pleasant Valley*. It was a beautiful book, full of life and vigor and happiness, written with the enthusiasm of a man who at forty had begun a new life, more rich and satisfying, if anything, than the life he had known as a youth.

In it, the ruined earth came to life and not only produced bounty, but provided Man with the roots and purpose in life he so desperately needed for renewal.

From then on, indeed, the constant theme of renewal became the key to my father's way of thinking. From *Pleasant Valley* and the books to follow about Malabar Farm it was easy to gather that for him nothing had become of greater importance than to create and renew life as long as life was left.

The Heritage

It was a powerful key which opened the minds of many men. And once *Pleasant Valley* was published, life at Malabar changed utterly, on the surface. From then on, there was seldom time for a walk down Switzer's Creek. But basically it made little difference, for the lesson had been learned and would never be forgotten.

11

The View from Mt. Jeez

My father followed up *Pleasant Valley* with two more books, *Malabar Farm* and *Out of the Earth,* each compiled from a new store of understanding and knowledge that had come to him from the years of continually deeper involvement with life on the farm. In chapters such as "Farming from Three to Twenty Feet Down" and "The World Can Feed Itself If It Wants To," he managed to describe the vast complexity of agriculture, which is at once a science, a business, a gamble and the basis for the survival and happiness of the world.

In other chapters, such as "The Farm Pond," he brought alive, in the quiet consideration of a spring pond from dawn until dusk, the small and fascinating world which exists and is multiplied time and again in every facet of farm life.

With the publication of these books, it didn't take long to discover that there were a great many people who shared my father's misgivings about the unstable, almost too dynamic, rootless rush of American life.

And there were others as concerned as he was about the manner in which, year after year, our soils were being depleted and our resources wasted by poor, unimaginative farming methods which had existed ever since our country's beginning, as if, indeed, there were still virgin soils to be squandered.

In a way it was surprising, in a time of constant pressure

of superficial distractions from thought, how many seemed to read *Malabar Farm* with eagerness and an innate longing. Perhaps we forget after all the permanence of values such as my father rediscovered. Man cannot live without satisfying those basic needs to use his hands and his brains and create the roots which bind him to the earth. My father was sure of it. And once they had read his point of view, there were many who, if they did not agree wholeheartedly with him, felt their own ideas akin enough to his to make them want to come and talk it over.

There were, of course, a liberal number of crackpots, who, having read his words, believed they had discovered a Messiah. Their letters provided exquisite dinnertime entertainment when the Boss, leaning back in his chair and decorously adjusting his reading glasses, quoted in reverent tones—"I want nothing more than to touch the hem of your garment"; or with the tremor of desperation in his voice, "What does it matter to me that you have a wife and three children? Nothing seems to matter any more"; or with a voluptuous moan, "Oh, I would I were a vampire bold!" This last went on interminably, in rhymed couplets. If the writer had made true her vows, we would undoubtedly have found the Boss, a marvelous spectacle for the tabloids, wrung dry and flung over a cliff somewhere with a couple of mysterious marks in his jugular vein. But the poor woman evidently hadn't the courage of her convictions and so remained, as her intended victim so often described her and her epistolary colleagues, "better imagined than seen."

As for the rest, the people who read *Pleasant Valley* and came to visit Malabar Farm seemed to be of a normal, hardworking, clear-minded sort. They were doctors, fascinated by the relationship of man's health to the soil. They were businessmen who, at my father's age, felt suddenly that they needed something more for their free time than a game of golf and drinks at the club. The greater number of them described their feeling as simply a desire for better understanding of humanity and life itself. They were not sure how this could be achieved, but they felt somehow that it had something to do with living closer to the land.

There were other businessmen, young and vigorous and able, who had found in *Pleasant Valley* a concern matching their own, which had to do with the isolation by great industrial cities of the workingman from the land and the very roots which could provide him with stability at any time regardless of the install-ment plan.

There were politicians with intense, busy, ambitious minds who loved to talk long into the night with a man who believed deeply that no soft comfort or governmental security was worth the price of a man's privilege to choose and direct his own life.

And there were farmers, tough-minded, experience-etched, hard-to-convince men who took every opportunity to needle the Boss mercilessly with facts and figures. And they were grateful to find someone who wrote of farming in a simple, sympathetic language which any man who had lived on and loved the land could understand immediately. And that is how the Sunday tours began.

The visitors would arrive in the morning, bringing their picnic lunches with them, prepared to spend the day. Out along the driveway would appear a line of vintage Fords, black and quaintly sedate, belonging to one sect of Mennonites, who were freer in their ways than those who insisted still on horse and carriage. They strode about in strange, tight old-fashioned trousers and lifeless gray shirts which, like the Fords, gave a sturdy romanticism to their strong bodies and sun-creased faces ringed by prophetic beards.

Up in the paddock, beyond the waving lines of laundry and a row of young blue Douglas firs, a hundred or more cars, up to their hub caps in bluegrass and sweet white clover, would be parked beside a couple of buses with banners across their sides declaring in bright red letters some such legend as "Jackson, Michigan, visits Louis Bromfield."

There in the early morning the visitors wandered at will, inspecting the beehives in a grove of butternut trees on the hill, looking over the hay loft, the cattle barn and milking parlor, testing the silage with critical experienced hands. When they had satisfied their curiosity as best they could, they sat down to eat their picnic lunches under the trees, respectfully scrupulous as farmers are about litter and paper or trampling of anything delicate and green. And, when they had drunk with a tin cup from the little faucet of cold spring water by the greenhouse, they settled patiently on the lawn to wait for the Boss to appear.

He was indoors, having his Sunday dinner amidst the racket of three or four simultaneous conversations, all shouted to be heard above the violent noise of *Traviata* roaring over the loudspeaker in the next room.

Perhaps Walter Pretzer, the greenhouse genius from Cleveland, a gentle, countrified man with a sharp, intelligent mind, was giving a discourse on the effect of liquid fertilizer on hothouse tomatoes.

At the same time, it was likely that Frank Lausche, who was then Governor of Ohio, was torturing the Boss with the obnoxious recollection that twice, during what was often referred to in our household as "the Roosevelt reign of tyranny," he had voted the straight Democratic ticket.

And, cutting across both conversations, George, his entire round little body shaking with disrespectful hilarity, was likely to be regaling a titled lady with a description of her leap from "barefooted Georgia Crackerdom" into Parisian society.

"Deny this!" With a triumphant cry that made his stiff, Balkan hair stand straight up on end, the Governor would produce some such incriminating evidence as a photo of my father and Mrs. Roosevelt apparently in intimate conversation.

"Hah! You had them stuck together! I know you crooked politicians through and through," my father would shout, leaping to his feet as if making ready for a heated speech of denial. But instead of uttering a further word on the subject and seemingly regarding his action as something unneedful of explanation, he would turn on his heel, leave his luncheon guests at the climax of their various conversations and stride through the front door onto the lawn.

The moment he appeared before the crowd, the man whose eyes in the past hour had been one moment blazing with fury and the next flooded with uncontrollable tears of laughter was completely transformed.

He became another self, one least seen by his closest friends and family: a calm, rational man, with sensible, perfectly-controlled emotions, apparently never upset by anything. It was quite obvious that this man never shouted. It was doubtful if he ever uttered a goddamn in his life. If anything about him was the same now, it was the quick, easy sense of humor and its accompanying natural charm, which even in moments of rage with us made him less frightening than he otherwise might have been.

He cut a romantic and yet gratifyingly authentic figure as he appeared, surrounded as always by his dogs and dressed as always in faded work clothes. Like Pa, if he could have thought the shenanigans of politics worth the trouble, he would have made a good politician, for people liked him immediately and, perhaps more important, he liked them. Often, in later years, when I heard George express doubt as to the worth of his exhausting himself by conducting these tours, which had increased from once on Sunday to twice and often every other day of the week as well, I heard my father give a reply, which from someone else might have sounded like hard-boiled, modern practicality. But coming from the Boss it only gave me a pang of rather poignant weariness. "You must realize one thing," he would say suddenly putting on what he must have thought to be the air of General Motors president at a board meeting, "every one of these people who come to listen to me on Sunday reads my books and buys them for his friends," and he would continue with a dreadful pomposity, "I can't afford to ignore them."

George's immediate reaction was invariably expressed in one all-inclusive word, "Nuts." For perhaps George knew better than anyone else that much as my father liked to envision himself as "capable of anything," shrewd business not excluded, he was nevertheless neither a businessman nor a salesman nor a politician. If he ever sold anything, it was because he believed in it with all his heart and mind. And if he came out to meet those gatherings of people on his lawn on Sunday afternoon, it was because he was grateful for and flattered by their recognition and because he was as interested in what they had come to talk over as they were. On no other basis could as ambitious, egotistical, thoughtful and curious a man as my father have talked so much and with such enthusiasm about one subject nearly every day for over eighteen years.

Sometimes he would sit down among the people on the broad sandstone steps that lead from the bountiful arms of Ganesha down across the lawn to the lower pastures. Sometimes, if the crowd was large, he would come around with the jeep, and leaning against it with a microphone in his hand, talk in a gentle, friendly voice which put everyone at ease.

For one like myself so used to his caged-lion antics within the household and the disrespectful results they gained, the way in which the crowd quieted at his first words never ceased to be amazing. It was as if the sound of the gentle, unassuming voice evoked a kind of loyal response from those around him so that the gossip and even the squalling of babies on the outer edge of the crowd came abruptly to an end.

"This is not a model farm," he would begin. "You have probably already noticed that there are no fancy white fences here, no registered cattle, no varnished stables. Nor is this an experimental station. We don't pretend to call ourselves scientists. We are simply farmers like yourselves, trying to combine a bit of book learning and modern theory with common sense and put the whole to practical use. One of our special prides here is that any operation in practice at Malabar can be carried out by any farmer of normal circumstances anywhere."

Then perhaps he would begin to talk about the manner in which our soils and resources were being drained by the "government-supported, lazy, unintelligent squanderings of bad farmers." Of how "poor land makes poor people" describing the listless migrant workers whose ancestors had systematically plundered the rich prairie until there was nothing left but the great dust bowl from which they were forced with their meager selves and meager possessions to take flight.

Or suddenly, it would become apparent that Walter Pretzer's quiet lecture had penetrated beneath the dinner-table racket earlier, as he launched on a well-informed description of the use of liquid fertilizer.

He was seldom accurate in his descriptions. If anything, he was expansive and grossly optimistic and I think any good farmer with sharp ears and a practical eye could have tripped him on a hundred disparities. But, somehow, his audience didn't seem to care about these enthusiastic exaggerations. What seemed to be important was the picture they evoked, the whole vast scene of farm life which suddenly became complete, important and, using one of his favorite expressions, "limitless in possibilities." The common everyday practice that most of those people carried out became suddenly alive and meaningful as he described them in a way that every farmer understood but could never quite describe to himself.

A dozen times during his talk some hard-bitten, weather-beaten old doubting Thomas must have been forced to say to himself, "Well, I never thought of it that way but—yes—it's true." And just when the old troublemaker, determined to discover some soft ground somewhere, prepared himself to snag the Boss with some such confidence-shattering question as "What you got down there on those lower fields that can't be seen from the road?" —my father would look him straight in the eye, grin disarmingly and say, "Perhaps some of you would like to take a quick look around?"

The "quick look around" required two things: undying enthusiasm and a staunch heart, for even in the punishing heat of midsummer it lasted the entire afternoon.

On one such tour, a poor old lady who had come especially to inspect our bird sanctuaries was sent flying into a swamp by five charging boxers, broke both ankles and had to be bedded down in the Big House for two weeks. Another time an old gentleman fainted from heat stroke and had to be revived with smelling salts on my mother's pink chaise longue.

But even if the flesh was vulnerable, enthusiasm seldom seemed to flag. It enabled garden club ladies, crackpots, Mennonites, grange masters, plain farmers and a good percentage of the population of Jackson, Michigan, to follow my father in a thick, rolling cloud of dust along a bumpy back road which led through every acre of cultivated land at Malabar Farm. Even the old rabble-rousing farmer with the constant look of doubt in his eyes must have been at least partially convinced of the Boss's knowledge of his land as, panting and wheezing, he paused to examine a clump of rich brown earth held out to him by the Boss, or to measure the height of a wheat field by the length of the Boss's own towering frame.

At last, just at dusk, when the sun had given up its furious attack on the human body and had relented in an almost conciliatory way, with a pale yellow light that seemed to flood the entire world with coolness and peace, my·father led his still faithful tribe to the top of Malabar Farm's highest hill.

George, who had little if any respect for the Sunday visitors and regarded their admiration of the Boss as irrational and silly as a religious fanatic's faith in the ultimate reward of heaven, named the big hill Mount Jeez, in honor of my father's weekly Sermons on the Mount.

Being a swearing family who never confused our cuss words with our Christian sentiments, we were never much troubled by a title which might have seemed sacrilegious to some. We liked it because we, too, liked to make fun of the Sunday visitors. But even if we hadn't, even if there had been no visitors and no sermons, there was something about the hill which once the name had been given could never quite justify casting it off. It gave a broad view of countless hills and forests which hinted temptingly of the untamed beauty lying beneath the trees and in the half-hidden valleys. Above the forest there was a distant glimpse of the wild, lonely Ferguson Place, forever secluded and reserved for the lonely dreams of men. And just below, bending toward Switzer's Creek and the heart of things, lay the low contoured fields of the farm, in broad, ribbonlike strips of bluegrass, alfalfa, yellow wheat and dark, vigorous corn, with here and there a tall white barn and a farm pond surrounded by feathery willows, fresh and cool and half asleep.

Since the day I left Malabar Farm for good, I have climbed many a mountain and looked down upon views more grand in many ways than the view from my father's highest hill. And yet, almost every time, looking out over the land from one or another high South American summit, I have felt a strange and, at first, inexplicable disappointment. Then suddenly a vivid memory comes to me of lying still between the grass and the sky of Mt. Jeez, looking down over my father's valley, and I have known where the difference lay. For only in a few places has there ever existed for me such a sense of devastating majesty and at the same time intimacy as in the view from Mt. Jeez.

Always in other vast scenes the sense of intimacy and civilization has somehow been overwhelmed by the huge, beautiful, parasitic wilderness, and the scene has become, rather than inspiring and reassuring, an unsettling reminder of man's continuous rift with nature. In the view from Mt. Jeez there was no such fearful sensation. Instead, one felt the continuing peace of man living in accord with the things about him. It was as if a truce had been made here between man and nature. As everywhere else, nature attacked Malabar with the heartless violence of a summer storm, intending to tear at the earth, washing it down the stream and leaving behind naked roots and the scars of open gullies. But here, man had curved the earth around the hills to hold the rain and water the plants and allow the roots to grow and secure the land. Nature, the aggressor, it seemed, had been impressed by this man's defense and somewhere in the midst of the battle one sensed that the two had become friends.

That was what I felt in my child's heart from the top of Mt. Jeez, and a great many saw what I saw, and, strangers though they were, must have felt something of what I felt. In the evening, they packed up their picnics at last and went away, some convinced, others skeptical still. Yet even the most doubting must have caught a glimpse, if only for a moment, of something far deeper and more satisfying than what life, on the surface, generally seems to provide.

My father had a simple way of putting it: "Of shallowness and dissatisfaction, happiness and a sense of accomplishment you get from life in exact degree the amount you give to it."

If the view from Mt. Jeez was proof of such a statement, it was credible enough. For to it he had given the best of everything he possessed.

 12

Christmas and the Three Witches

He called them the three witches. I can't tell exactly why, nor does it seem to matter, for without further explanation and without any real desire to disparage, the title seemed to suit them. He swore that they spent their lives plotting for his possession, but that would have been quite unnecessary, since, considering everything, they possessed him already. To deprive him of the things they stood for would have been to deprive him of his gaiety, his delightful sense of the ridiculous—the very things that sparked his imagination. There would have been nothing left of him but purposefulness, dedication and the kind of nasty warped ego that makes demagogues; for, after all, what else is left when a smart, ambitious man hasn't got a sense of humor?

But thank Heaven, just as much as he belonged to the Friends of the Land, the Ohio Wildlife Commission, the Cleveland Heights Garden Club and the National Vegetable Growers Association, he belonged to those three incredibly steadfast ladies who presided over Christmas at Malabar.

I could not have been more than four when I saw Gene for the first time. Leaning from the window of the nursery of the Presbytère on one of those restless Sunday afternoons, I caught sight of her sitting on the terrace, her pleasant figure brightly etched against a background of potted geraniums and ageratums, chatting comfortably with Madame de Fresené in the most appalling French. Madame de Fresené didn't seem to mind her lack of finesse—in fact she seemed to be enjoying it, responding cheerfully, laughing and leaning toward Gene as one leans toward the first morning rays of the sun as if better to absorb their perfect pleasantness. Perhaps she felt as I did at that moment that she had never seen anyone so pretty in her life and that what Gene said didn't matter because the special comfort of her presence was enough.

There was something of angelic innocence in the aureole softness of her honey-colored hair above a smooth forehead and delicate china-blue eyes. But there the heavenliness ceased as those eyes slanted and cheekbones and mouth curved prettily upward with the feline beauty of a plump Persian kitten who, seated by a fire or stretched in the sunshine of a terrace, quite unmindfully and without caring one way or the other, lends a languid ease and warmth to everything about her.

The attitude suited her perfectly, the entire atmosphere in which she lived lent itself to pleasure, ease and indifference. In those days, she lived the delightfully pampered life of a rich New York heiress: a life of Fifth Avenue shops, the theater, cocktails and long, marvelous holidays on the Continent.

Since those careless days in the early thirties she had seen a great deal of tragedy. She had outlived a doting husband and, in the battle of Normandy, lost her only son without ever having had, in her gay, busy life, the opportunity to know him. Quite certainly, in that moment, she must have discovered in a most brutal manner how harsh and terrible the world can be. Many of tougher fiber would have been defeated by the experience, but Gene's nature led her along a different and unexpected course. As if by some miracle, after her son's death she became "clairvoyant" and with her new "gift of insight" spent hours and days and months visiting the hospitals of the most tragically wounded, telling fortunes and with the gay spirit of a spoiled angel bringing laughter and thus hope into the most helpless and hopeless hearts.

Still, the most remarkable thing in all this was not the course she took, but the manner in which she refused to allow it to change her role in the world.

"How their faces light up, the poor darlings," she would say of her wounded boys as if she were quite unaware of how the miracle of their smiles came about. Nor did she add, "It's worth all the trouble just for that," as if she had calculated the price and accepted her martyrdom. No, it was just as, when years later, seated at lunch at Pierre's, she suddenly leaned toward me in her gay, bland manner and chuckled delightedly, "By the way, Ellie dear, you won't believe it, but I've been made chief of my division of the Salvation Army. Isn't that the most insane thing you've ever heard?"

On the surface, it did seem a bit unbalanced, for who on earth would have imagined such a delightfully addle-headed creature as Gene being aware of "the Army's" existence, unless it was as the subject of a good *New Yorker* cartoon. But that, of course, was why at that moment I felt an intense pang of affection for her. She had become neither dowdy nor preachy nor dedicated nor any of the other frightful things that might have happened. Indeed, the idea that she was working for the Salvation Army was as amusing to her as it might have been to anyone who had known her in the thirties.

Thus, when she sat in her special corner of the sofa at Malabar Farm on Christmas Eve, she seemed not to have changed at all. She was, if anything, more than ever like a comfortable Persian cat grown plump with age, still effortlessly dispensing warmth and good humor, still seemingly unaware that the world was a hard and troublesome place to live in. And when my father caught sight of that minxlike face, prettier than ever, the look in his eyes was so full of mixed emotions evoked by the present and the past that one wondered whether he would laugh aloud or go off somewhere and, all by himself, weep in gratitude.

Gene was one fragment left perfectly intact from those happy Sunday afternoons at the Presbytère. Annie was another.

There was something in the very healthy, animal beauty of Annie that made us delight in the fact that she could never seem to make any sort of order of the incredible tangle of loose ends that were her life. Something in her blond rosiness, and exciting allure in her eyes, a certain overall untidiness which seemed to emanate as much from within as from without, made her doubly attractive. Every time her noisy laughter, which sounded as though it belonged to an English pub, rang through the hum and babble of the Sunday afternoon, it was certain that somewhere in some heart Annie had made a life-long conquest. It was simply the way she was; one loved her more for what she shouldn't have done than for what she should.

How often I heard that laugh in all my growing years; for always she seemed indeed to be far more a part of the Presbytère than of the ancient household around the corner and up the street where she lived with her tragically humorless French-Egyptian husband and two lively, if bewildered, little boys. My father was forever settling her life, and if the end result of his advice provided a better story than it did a solution, it mattered little; for it was the laughter they derived from their constant schemings that counted in this, and not the life that one way or another was preordained to be chaotic.

Annie, like Gene, was an American abroad, part of the strange rootless crowd of international society that had fascinated, delighted and appalled my father for so many years. When war came and we returned to America, she came as well, discarding her difficult husband on the way and bringing the boys to Malabar Farm to stay for an "indefinite period" while it was decided what should be done with their lives.

The "indefinite period" lasted some sixteen years until all

was precipitously resolved by their growing into young men. In the meantime, Annie became a career woman in the world of fashion and, among other things, what she called in amused commercialese "A Christmas Shopping Counseler." Since she delighted in extravagance and had a wry sense of humor, she did very well: buying toy motor cars that were "certain suicide" for horrid, spoiled little boys, expensive jewels for dissatisfied wives and naughty negligees for old men's darlings.

When at last there was a pause in the frenzy of festive purchasing, she came out to the farm to attend to the boys. The boys called her "Our Mother" with the kind of cautious reverence attributed to otherworldly creatures not quite believed in; and when my father announced in portentous tones: "Better clean up your fingernails, Our Mother's coming," they became oddly silent with a mingling of excitement, unreasoning hope and dread.

The moment she arrived at Malabar, she washed their mouths with soap in an effort to purge them of all the swear words learned in our presence and then, locking herself in with them, lectured them incessantly for three days and three nights.

In all the years that Christmas at Malabar brought us together, Annie's life was as it had been from the beginning, beset by disaster, financial upset and the kind of endless precariousness that causes gamblers to end up drunk and broke in garrets. And yet, the last time I saw her, in Christmas, 1951, she was still the same handsome, boisterous girl with the bawdy barroom laugh I had known in the garden in France, and I am positive she still is.

The third witch was La Beth. Like the others, of course, I knew her first at the Presbytère, where, before going off to dinner in Paris, she would come to sit in the nursery clothed in an evening gown that resembled an elegant blue satin nurse's uniform, with a bird of Paradise balancing worriedly atop her head as she read the Sunday funnies in birdlike tones, with broad *a*'s that seemed to have slipped in among the notes of her great shipping inheritance. She made a formidable list of "dates" on the phone, ordered her Rolls-Royce, and, in general, commented on all that "ought to be done."

"'I mean *really*," she would protest, "something ought to be done about Annie's face (at the moment she simply has none)"; or "Louis's smoking; his fingers look as though he dealt in the opium trade"; or "those awful blizzards that come up the minute I arrive in the country, I mean *really*."

The conception that something could be done about a blizzard came easily to Beth, for since the day, in heaven knows what century, that she had gone to live at the Hotel St. Regis, it had only been necessary for her to pick up the phone for someone to do something about something. There was Sidney, "my boy friend who looks after the theater tickets," and Patrick, who knew all sorts of things everyone else had long since forgotten about the Rolls-Royce, and Gene, who knew just when to turn the steak at the Colony. J. Edgar watched over her with the solicitude of an after-hours sleuth; Jim Farley took care of her politics. She called them all "my boy friends" with a coy manner, in spite of which one look at her iron-bound countenance would have dispelled all naughty speculations.

With such an entourage to set things in order, it was inevitable that she should be a creature of habit. She never changed the size of her shoes (doggedly denying growth after the age of ten), the uniformlike pattern of her dresses and her cockatoos, nor the style of her raven black hair. Half of every evening she spent at El Morocco and the other half at the Stork, abstaining rigidly from dance, drink and tobacco while she sat like an ancient potentate at her "special table," bobbing her feathers and keeping someone dashing from table to table with greetings, written hurriedly, ever so hurriedly—in her dry, concise, bejeweled little hand.

Christmas and the Three Witches

She wintered in New York, spent spring in Paris and often summered in Biarritz, and wherever she went she took along her collection of hats and photographs of all the world's people worth knowing. Select as it was, the collection took up so much space in her spacious St. Regis apartment that one could never sit down and toss one's hat carelessly across the sofa without danger of being buried under an avalanche of the Pope, the Duchess of Kent, Vincent Astor, William Vanderbilt and Joan Fontaine.

Annie's and Gene's were not among the photos of people worth knowing, and since, like most of the people who had once met on Sundays at the Presbytère, they never met except in the presence of the Bromfields, each of them arrived at Mansfield station on a different train. I suppose this helped to preserve that much longer the illusion that this year the other two had fallen out of favor and, at last, had not been invited. The illusion was shattered the moment they reached the farm and were forced to greet one another with little exclamations of hurt surprise.

"Why, daahling, why didn't you *tell* me you were coming? I would have been *so* much more cozy. Traveling alone *is* such a bore."

If there was wounded dignity in their tone at having thus been evaded, there was, at the same time, consternation: a kind of patent hint that if the truth had been known a trip to Colorado Springs could have been arranged instead. Nor were they alone in this little drama of their meeting, for which they had no doubt been mentally rehearsing all night on the train. The moment my father announced with a loud, phony groan, "I suppose there's no way out of having the Three Witches for Christmas," my mother began to dread their arrival with the same appalled anticipation that she had dreaded the Sunday lunches long ago at the Presbytère. Each time she held out her trembling hands or proffered a kiss, her eyes held a veiled look of skepticism, amusement and terror, remembering what one had said of the other two the last time she had met them all *separately* in New York.

And yet, once their greeting was disposed of, it didn't take long for them to be seated around the big fire in the living room, gossiping avidly as if they were the oldest and best of friends, which, if they would admit it, once a year indeed they were.

Since in New York they never failed to cross the street to avoid one another, it was a strange sort of gossip, related entirely to the past and the only world that had ever succeeded in bringing them together. And so, as they warmed to their memories and thus to one another, an odd thing began to happen. Suddenly in that big comfortable room with its books and star-spangled mirror and familiar furniture, one had the sensation that, by opening the tall French doors, instead of letting in the chilled winter air, one could expect the scent of lilacs and the gay and cryptic babble of a Sunday afternoon to drift in on a warm summer breeze. The past, a bit musty and dated, seemed to rise with a kind of delightful ghostly insanity, as Gene with a mysterious little smile leaned toward my mother and resurrected some incredible relic.

"Mary daahling, you'll never dream who suddenly appeared before my eyes the other day!"

A dubious smile would cross my mother's face. "That horrible, sentimental old nurse of yours? Did you weep buckets?"

"Oh, no, nothing so pure and sweet as that. No, just imagine— the Princess Leblonsky."

"Never! You mean that old Russian Hessian with the dirty diamonds?"

"Exactly! Do you remember those fantastic parties in Paris with four orchestras and her grand stairway lined with Nubian slaves wearing nothing but bowls of fruit?"

"How could anyone forget? She used to receive her guests in a kind of red velvet gown with all sorts of supports inside so that when she bowed you felt as though she were offering up her bosom in a pearl-encrusted goblet."

"My God." Annie would cross one handsome leg across another and give a malevolent little grin. "Did you get a close look at her? It must have been terrifying. What is she up to? Did she say?"

"To tell the truth, dear, she seemed to be avoiding me—you know how *dreadfully snobbish* some of those people who used to come to Senlis on Sundays could be. We only smiled at one another rather vaguely—but even from a great distance she looked covered with jewels and expensively dressed as ever!"

"Do you think she can really still afford the life she had in France?" Beth, whose piety had been temporarily affronted by the word "bosom," would be now unable to suppress a new point of speculation. "She's the only rich White Russian I've ever known, and so frightfully ugly. I just can't imagine where she finds the means. Unless, of course, it's true what a boy friend of mine once hinted to me, that she was the one who made off with the Russian Crown Jewels."

"Christ knows, she's crafty enough, if you're talking about who I think you are!" My father came into the room suddenly, dripping melting snow behind him, and looked down with an air of incredulous and delighted astonishment at Beth. "That get-up is not true. Nobody could have invented it!"

Beth, who was garbed in a combination of baby blue rompers, a flowered plastic apron, a sequined, spangled cloche hat and long black evening gloves which did indeed merit astonishment, would regard her inquisitor with a calm, challenging expression. "It most certainly *is* true, and extremely practical, if you ask me."

With an agitated sweep of her black-gloved hand she would gesture toward her surroundings. "Perhaps you don't notice that every time you fling open that front door the temperature drops to fifty below. *I* have a delicate head. I cawn't stand it. And the dawgs! I've never sat down to a meal without all seven of them coming to rest their drooling jowls on my knees. You'll have to admit it's not very pleasant."

"Not pleasant—*you* ought to be flattered. Still, I do see the great practicality of the apron and I really think it's heroic, this great revolution after thirty years of nothing but Harrods' royal blues. But that doesn't explain the gloves. Don't tell me you've become a hypochondriac like Lady Fitzsimmons, who had to have the door knobs in all the hotels polished with alcohol before she'd touch them."

"Heavens, no. It's the newsprint on these village papers," Beth would groan, holding the Chicago *Tribune* out as an example. "Do you know what my boy friend, the doorman, said to me when I arrived home after Christmas last year? When I took off my gloves, he said, 'Been out to the mining country, Miss Leary?' Now I ask you, the dawman of awl people. So I said to myself, this time when I leave the safety of the civilized world I'll see that I keep my hands clean."

Having thus classified Malabar Farm, she would look up again to discover that the lines of weariness and frustration on my father's face, which had shown themselves a moment ago in spite of his growing amusement, had all dissolved now into a mass of laugh wrinkles. A new vigor kindled by more than the fresh wintry morning would come into his eyes. And even if Beth never suspected it under the dubious protection of her ridiculous spangled beanie, a feeling of gratitude must have passed between them for the fact that, in spite of all the things that had happened during their lives, she could still be sitting before him, as she had sat in the nursery at the Presbytère, reading the funnies with the scent of lilacs and Annie's shrieks of laughter coming through the open windows above the dying babble of Sunday's departing guests.

Somehow, it suddenly did seem as if all had been only yesterday and there had been nothing in between. For a brief time, the

Friends of the Land, the Ohio Wildlife Commission and all those other devoted institutions ceased to exist and my father plunged into a fine selfish holiday of reading, writing, listening to music, gossiping, dancing, playfully recalling a life that had been perhaps too gay and untroubled and perfect in its way to be real. He could have taken a trip anywhere, rested for a month in some luxurious resort and felt only that he was wasting time. None of it would have brought back his vigor and good humor —his very sanity—half so well as the presence in his house of the Three Witches and the incredible, hilarious memories they revived, which made him turn to his daughters and say, "You've never lived and you never will because you didn't know the twenties."

Then turning to Gene he chuckled reminiscently, "Remember M. Bonnet, who kept his wife's ashes in an oriental urn in the salon?"

"But, of course, daahling, didn't that dreadful woman, the Duchess de Mt. Claire, sniff them all up as snuff?"

"Aah, but what he said to her when he discovered what she'd done was one of the most magnificent condemnations I've ever heard." Drawing himself up and glaring at Gene with tragic Gallic pomposity, my father would pronounce gravely, "Madame, vous êtes la tombe de ma femme."

When they had made the most of the Duchess de Mt. Claire, they would go on to some other equally implausible object of laughter. It might have been Miss Lucretia Merriweather, who built bird's nests and came to her end by falling from an immense hand-made oriole's nest and breaking her neck. It might have been the Right Honorable Lady Bainsbury, who kept a smooth and girlish skin by taking injections of wax, until one especially hot afternoon at the Presbytère, when, in a most unfortunate manner, all the wax melted into her chin.

There was no end to the tales once they had begun and though we had heard most of them any number of times—

because they were good stories, the basis of many of the best tales my father ever put into print—we never tired of listening to them.

Indeed it was Anne, Hope and I who now sometimes seemed to live in a world bound by the same hills that bound the world of my father's childhood. And, oddly enough, this nonsense we heard at the dinner table and in the long evenings by the fire was better able at times to lift us and carry us beyond those narrow boundaries than all the good music and books at our disposal. The Three Witches were like a proof of the pudding, every bit as fantastic and vivid and extreme as the characters in a good novel, and a certain alchemy began to work the moment they came in contact with the tireless imagination of my father, which made them more wonderful to us than they might have been had we met at some other time and place on our own. They taught us a valuable lesson: that no matter how some may try to make it so, the world is not commonplace. It is rich in surprises and full of great and good and terrible moments, which, in the end, outweigh the commonplace on any scale.

Everyone at Malabar, family and visitors alike, were touched by this alchemy at Christmas. There were always others there, newspaper people, tired and depressed from a tour of the war front, as badly in need of fun and nonsense as my father; high school boys who helped with the summer haying and somehow couldn't resist their curiosity about winter at Malabar Farm; and generally two or three young fliers whom George and the Boss had met on some bond tour or other. For them this was wonderful respite from the dread and horror and uncertainty of war.

What must they have thought when suddenly, in the midst of dinner, George leapt to his feet and stretching his stocky bull's neck and curving his chubby, dexterous fingers, gave a fantastically credible imitation of some ancient, renowned Indian dancer? How must they have taken it when my father, his head shrouded in a white linen dinner napkin with two large lumps of sugar protruding grotesquely from beneath his upper lip, eyes flashing murderously, knife raised, lunged at Beth in his classical portrayal of the "Mad Nun"?

Sometime afterward, when they were on some terrible or terrifying mission, I like to believe that they remembered the lunatic behavior of their Christmas hosts and that, if they survived the war, they, like ourselves, could never again be made to believe that the world was worth living in without laughter.

Of course, even during the winter holiday there were supposed to be one or two serious moments: such as, for example, the morning on which Annie elected to have her annual conference with the Boss on the pressing subject of "What ought to be done with the boys."

Inevitably she tried to catch him while he was still in bed, a maneuver which was not so erratic as it may have seemed, considering that everyone from Max Drake, with a new program for the dairy, to Mrs. Byerly, the laundress, come to tell him about Sam drinking up the pension, never failed to use exactly the same tactics. It was the hour he devoted, with his first cup of coffee, to reading the *New York Times,* the *Tribune,* the *Daily News* and *Mirror,* Washington *Post,* Cleveland *Plain Dealer,* Cleveland *Press,* the Toledo *Blade* and the Mansfield *News Journal.* Such a cumbersome mountain of reading matter had a certain stabilizing effect. Anyone who spent any time at Malabar Farm soon discovered that as long as it all rested on or about my father's knees it was possible to find him in one place, while the rest of the time it wasn't.

On this assumption, Annie would tiptoe down the front stairs in all their empty grandeur of early morning and, like everyone else, thrust open his bedroom door unannounced.

It was often difficult to locate him beneath the newspapers, coffee cups, ash trays full of discarded cigarette butts and three or four dogs holding snarling vigilance over an empty cornflakes bowl. But once she had found him, Annie cleared herself a modest place at the bottom right-hand corner of his bed and faced him with an unusual look of urgency, "Now, Lou, I *insist* we get something settled about Tony and Patrick."

The pile of debris rumbled and trembled as my father struggled to rise. At last, above the mountain of his newspaper-covered knees, his face would appear, as old and all-knowing and martyred with the world's troubles as the face of Krishna.

"God knows, it's about time. Although," the room would suddenly seem suffocating with ominousness, "it's not going to be simple."

"But, Lou," Annie would rattle, cheerfully racing toward the finish before the Boss could break in with some disheartening protest, "it *will* be simple, I've got it all arranged with Mr. Hannah—you know the dear old man—they can go right into Western Reserve at the beginning of the new term. Really, there'll be nothing to it, we'll just pop them in, and out they'll come at the end of the first term, two *marvelous* little gentlemen. It's a wonderful place—I stopped there on my way here—full of school spirit and tradition and discipline and perfect little gentlemen walking around everywhere. Well!" Only then did she gasp for breath. "That's settled. It's such a relief to have it all taken care of once and for all."

"Hurruuumph!" The room was now so heavy with foreboding that it must have taken all Annie's will not to rush out into the garden for air. "On the surface it sounds fine, but what about the Jesuit College and St. Paul's? How did they come out of that? And what *is* dear old Mr. Hannah going to say when Tony fails his first exam? Listen, Annie," with a sorrowful look, my father would sit up among the pillows and brace himself with the air of an unwilling witness, "I really don't want to upset you but there are a few things I'm afraid

I'm going to have to tell you about the boys, things that are really nothing to joke about. Now take, for example, what happened the other night. I know boys will be boys, but I'd call this beyond normal behavior. I'd call it, well," a moment's hesitation made my father's pronouncement all the more dramatic, "sinister. . . ."

Pausing again to see if Annie's anxiety was mounting properly, he would go on, "Christ. They stuffed their beds with dummies, climbed up on the roof and rang the dinner bell. At midnight! All hell broke loose, of course. Mary ran through the house bellowing, 'Fire!' The farm manager came running with a gun, Nanny nearly got shot and caught her death of cold trying to rescue them from a hail of buckshot."

In an instant, the gloom that had pervaded the air would be shot through with one of Annie's unrivaled shrieks of laughter. "Thank God, thank God, for that. They *do* have a sense of humor. You have no idea the agonies I've suffered thinking they'd turn out as dull and humorless as their father. Oh, do go on. . . . Then what happened?"

As Annie leaned eagerly toward him, her eyes sparkling with relief and delight, my father's big shoulders would begin to shake as somewhere deep in his chest a sudden uncontrollable hilarity battled momentarily with the effects of too much tobacco and made its way to the surface, "I found Mary hysterical with rage, frantically beating the dummies with Patrick's shoe. Good God, how I wish you'd been there! It reminded me suddenly of how you held César's Ming Dynasty vase above your head and threatened to smash it if he didn't give you the trip to India."

"Alors, it worked, didn't it? That damned hideous vase was worth more than my boat fare there and back. Oh, heavens, Louis, when you think back over it, no wonder the poor dears are a bit unstable. But never mind! What matters, thank God," she repeated, laughing again with pleasure and pride, "is that they *do* have a sense of humor."

"Well, yes, I'll admit they do. And it's a damn good thing. Life would be a hell of a mess without . . ." All at once it would seem impossible even to philosophize, let alone be severe, "Do you remember the time you actually did smash that God-awful aquarium bar of his?" Tears of hilarity wrung themselves from my father's eyes. "That was one of the funniest evenings of my life. You and César screaming at one another up to your knees in water and that harridan of your mother-in-law crawling about on her hands and knees collecting fish in the Louis XV porcelain vase."

For quite a while it would go on like this, the two laughing uproariously, until my father glanced at his watch with a stricken look. "Christ, I enjoyed myself so much I lost track of the time. Look—I promised the children I'd go and hunt for a tree. Damned nuisance, but I must get it. Annie, about the boys. We'll have to talk about it more, of course, another time. In the meantime, this business of school—perhaps another year . . ."

That was just one conference held on a crisp winter morning, full of the excitement of Christmas and not in the least conducive to serious thought and the settling of young men's lives. There would be sixteen more of the same before, as I have already mentioned, the boys, in spite of their "sinister" behavior, turned into normal, intelligent, well-balanced men with the right amount of common sense and good humor to carry them through. In the meantime, my father went out to look for a Christmas tree.

He found it at the most distant part of the farm, called the Nimen Place, on the edge of a spring pond where, at Malabar's beginning, we had planted a grove of Scotch firs close together so that every year at Christmastime we might take a tree, and leave a space for the other trees to grow. We brought it home along the snow-laden road by tractor and wagon and dragged it through the front door to its place between the twin staircases, where for the last days of its life it would stand in gaudy magnificence, its highest branch with a star rising above the second landing, shedding an extravagant, gay brilliance over a joyful household.

Its decoration was a busy, complicated affair which involved running up the stairs, swinging from the banister with a lot of tinsel and sliding back down again. There were so many "experts" putting the right ornament in the exactly right spot that the final effect was exactly as it should have been, a mayhem of sparkling light and color, warm and friendly and happily defiant of all attempt at symmetry. If my father had had an aesthetic impulse at the start it would have been totally destroyed by the new lights Nanny had discovered at Woolworth's. They resembled syringes with colored water inside thin cylinders which boiled and bubbled constantly in upward spirals. No one wished to hurt Nanny's feelings by not using them, but George neatly put a damper on any intention of buying more of them with a single comment that, had it reached the proper ears, would have put the bubble industry out of business overnight. "Farts in a bathtub," he called them, and went calmly about his business of trimming the tree.

When the work was finished at last, the Boss sank into his place at the card table with a double shot of whiskey, as if settled, exhausted and immovable for the evening. But, after a time, through the noise and laughter and argument over the cards, the sound of *Les Sylphides* or *Firebird* would force its way with the subtle irrepressibility of beauty into his awareness, and his long cigarette-stained fingers would begin to dance above his head with a peculiar grace, recalling the exact motions of Markova in London in 1936. Then in the midst of the game, he would rise and go into the hall.

We children flew after him and, for the rest of the evening, the hall became a gay, undisciplined annex of Covent Garden. While we whirled and pirouetted and leapt and made adoring fun of Markova and Lichine, Beth sat alone thinking of the midnight mass at St. Patrick's, which in all the years of Malabar's existence she had thrown over. For what? Icy gales, dirty newsprint and dogs drooling on a plastic apron.

In a corner of the sofa, Gene sat with the cards spread before her, smiling happily over the wonderful things they revealed to be in store for the young airman who, the day after tomorrow, would be headed for California and then only heaven could know where.

"There's a long journey here to a place you've never seen before (that's where you're headed for, of course). And here— here's a lovely girl, dark-haired—I don't know quite where you'll meet her. Could be one of those *divine* South Sea Island beauties. Oh no, really this is *too* exciting—you'll *definitely* have a love affair and perhaps—well—it looks as if you may get hooked. Daahling, can you imagine yourself king of a South Sea Island? Oh, really, it's all so exciting, such an adventure, so Somerset Maughamish."

Just about the time that the last little bell from St. Patrick's had tinkled its faint reprimand in Beth's ear, George, who had gone upstairs after the decorating—apparently to sleep off a drop too much vodka—would reappear at the head of the stairs: a sleep-swollen Christmas angel all in the white of his perpetual toweling bathrobe, hair standing on end, a candle clasped, with fraudulent angelic sweetness, just above his ample middle.

By a series of well-executed pirouettes he made his way down the stairs and resting his candle on the piano beckoned in a voice half persuasive, half commanding, "Annie."

From somewhere behind an old scrapbook of India, Annie appeared, dressed in a ski costume, which at the time of Theda Bara's debut must have been the height of chic, and pranced lightly, pursued by George, through an intricate and naughty performance of *Afternoon of a Faun*.

From time to time from the staircase where she had settled herself to watch the goings-on, my mother could be heard to chirp nervously, "Oops—alors, prenez garde les enfants." But she needn't have bothered, for "les enfants," unable to stand or sit any longer, had collapsed, as children should, in the nursery upstairs. By the time we awoke again and crept downstairs, the house was enveloped in utter silence and all that was left of last evening's gaiety was a rotund figure in a white toweling bathrobe stretched out before the Christmas tree, his hands in sepulchral repose across his middle. Four candles, two at his head and two at his feet, flickered peacefully in the last gray light of Christmas dawn.

 13

Death of a Critic

Eager as we were to begin opening the presents on Christmas
Day, we didn't waken George immediately, but beckoned to
Nanny and Annie's boys to come, and for a long time the six
of us sat on the stairs in fits of muted giggles.

Somehow, without quite knowing why, we wanted this ridiculous moment to last as long as possible. Of course, the grotesque
and comic spectacle delighted and enchanted us all. But beyond
that, I sometimes can't help wondering if somewhere, deep in
our hearts and in some hidden corner of our minds, we didn't
feel a strange need to put off awakening George for just a moment
longer, to postpone the reality of the end of Christmas Day.
After that, the Three Witches would return to the life in which
they declined to know one another; and with a serious purposefulness that, like a poorly tailored suit, never seemed to "hang together right" in spite of its fine cloth, the Boss would return to
the role of an agricultural prophet.

It was quite natural, of course, this return to the world of purpose. For as surely as he was born to tell tales, my father was born
as well with farmer's blood. And just as it was inevitable that he
should turn to the land, so it was that, with his ability to write
and his incessant ambition to be known, he should become probably the most famous farmer in the world.

I suppose in the end it is for his readers to decide whether the things he wrote of the land and its relation to man and the universe caused his talent for writing to be of greater value than ever, or whether his preoccupation with these things simply diluted the ink and spoiled the career of an excellent story-teller.

About the latter opinion, no one was more adamant than George Hawkins. If, from the depths of his grave, George should somehow hear that, after a period of adjustment, *Malabar Farm* and *Out of the Earth* were selling more copies than *The Rains Came* and *Mrs. Parkington,* I am quite sure that he would rise up and without the slightest consideration of impending heavenly wrath, shout, "Goddamn the phony, pompous sons of bitches! How dare they?" For such was George's opinion of anyone who would prefer reading my father's agricultural and philosophical writings to one of his "damn good novels."

George had no innate desire to improve the world. He felt that it was good enough as it stood, as long as one picked and chose one's pleasures in the right places and didn't look for trouble. In accordance with this reasoning, after a day of typing *Malabar Farm* or *Out of the Earth,* he would strip the book of all the beauty and romanticism it possessed by pronouncing in exhausted tones, "Here's your humus, mucus, retch and vetch, all 140 pages of it and that, thank Christ, is that."

Among us all, George was the only one who never acquired more than the most perfunctory attachment for Malabar Farm. From one day to the next, he could have packed his suitcase and gone off to Hollywood or New York or France to pick up the old threads and continue his life of fun and ease and adventure as though it had never ended. It had been the perfect life for him. His heart and mind sought no further satisfaction.

But he needed us too. And so he remained, typing that "Goddamn humus, mucus, retch and vetch" having the best time he could (which one must admit was generally not bad at all) and living in constant fear that my father might one day come to take himself too seriously, thus losing his sense of humor and balance to such a degree that he became nothing but a "dreadful hogwash preaching old bore."

To avoid so unthinkable an end, George used all the talents with which nature had so lavishly endowed him. When the members of one garden club or another, picture-hatted, high-heeled, wobbly-buttocked embodiments of emancipated womanhood all, came full of tittering excitement to spend the day at Malabar, George gave them what he graphically described as "the treatment." Peering through our dining-room windows with a mingling of coy and authoritative matronly boldness, the ladies inevitably found their view blocked by the short, swarthy, mustached figure of a madman who, hair standing on end, screwed up his face in a wild and ghastly manner. With little breathless "ohs" and "ahs" they would move on to another window, but there he was again, grimacing, sticking out his tongue, thumbing first his ears and then his nose. There was, it seemed, no alternative for the ladies but to move away from this dreadful spectacle and go to sit on the lawn, where they might recompose themselves, catch their breath and ask one another if what they had seen was really true! But before there was time to find some excuse for the presence of this rude lunatic in the midst of what they had expected from their perusal of *Pleasant Valley* to be a sunlit, tranquil scene, he appeared again, this time with his large brown stomach dubiously enveloped in a pair of loud Scotch plaid bathing trunks. Bowing slightly and showing two rows of wolfish yellow teeth in a servile smile, he would announce, "God will be with you in a moment." Then, dragging a lawn chair into the center of the gathering and plumping himself into it, he would promptly fall asleep.

When "God" did appear in a moment, it was to discover that his warmly dedicated talk on soil conservation had somehow lost a great deal of its effect to the incongruous presence of a fat, naked Buddha-like figure, who, hands crossed peacefully across his middle, sat oblivious to the prophetic words of the master, contentedly dozing in the sun.

He was not blindly indiscriminate in his judgment of the new and unfamiliar characters who came to surround the Boss. There were among the rugged, red-faced old farmers who used to ask of him with a searching, suspicious look, "Whar's the mentolit?" a great many of whom he became amusedly and even respectfully fond. And there were even some whom, after a few preliminary goadings, he allowed without further interruption to have their say concerning what he considered to be the highly overrated subject of soil conservation. But they had to have the subtle, delightful humor of Frank Lausche or the great blustering power and character of Big Hugh Bennett, the quiet candor of Dr. Paul Sears or Grove Patterson of the Toledo *Blade*. For his acceptance and even love of these dedicated conservationists and first-class citizens of the United States, he earned adoration and the delightful acceptance of his jibes in return. I suppose even they, from time to time, were glad of the touch of the ridiculous he contributed to their more serious moments. They were all men who loved heartily to laugh.

But there were others of a less flamboyant caliber whom George considered a waste of time and summarily grouped under the heading of "gland types." Their unblinking devotion to my father was, in his words, "vomit making." The moment he spied the arrival of a "gland type" from the same dining-room window, through which he'd just recently thumbed his nose at a gathering of ladies from Cleveland Heights, he made a rapid retreat to his room, where he spent the rest of the day nursing an angry sense of intrusion with glasses of milk and large slices of bread spread amply with butter and garlic. Nor did he emerge until he was quite sure of their departure. Then, descending the stairs with an air of great martyrdom, he would seat himself on the sofa in the living room, adjust his glasses and, taking up the *Daily Mirror*, inquire from behind it with a somehow illogical indifference, "Well, what the hell did those phony bastards get out of you today?" My father would glare, and George would add with finality, "If it's another of those insane conservation tours, count me out. You can tramp around in the rain, smelling silage and squeezing soil samples and eating those interminable barbecues and hush puppies fried in rancid oil all you like. I've drawn the line." And before my father could answer, "Who asked you to come along?" he would, having had his say, abruptly toss down the newspaper and march back to bed.

It was this very boldness, of course, this "nothing to lose" attitude, that made George intentionally or unintentionally, my father's greatest friend. We all need someone near us who is totally unafraid of us, whose power of criticism can be as boundless as his power to praise; and to the brittle, pitiless face George presented him I am sure my father confided more rage, grief, happiness and satisfaction than to anyone else on earth. In response George neither cringed before rage, nor demonstrated before success any sign of the sentimentality my father so despised and feared. He struck back at my father's tirades with all sorts of weapons from practical jokes and tirades of his own to the flinging of ski boots and whiskey bottles.

He could thrust a manuscript under the Boss's nose and roar with the indignation of an enraged bull, "You don't mean to sit there and tell me you expect me to type *this* crap! I never read such uninhibited corn in my life!"

And yet, in another moment, I can hear him say in a matter-of-fact tone all the more touching for its marked carelessness, "You know, Lou, that stuff you handed me this morning is damned good. Goldwyn would sink a pile into that. If I were you, I wouldn't change a thing."

My father might answer in either case, "What in hell do you know about it, you lousy, third-rate Hollywood hack?" Still, in the back of his mind, I'm sure he was all attention, for he knew that George understood. Better than anyone, he knew my father's mind.

And yet I am just as certain none of us, not even my father, ever really knew what went on in the mind of George Hawkins. He had spent nearly a quarter of a century with us, amusing us, listening to our troubles, driving us to the brink of homicide with his intrigue, leading us into fantastic escapades.

But whether he truly cared for us or had ever cared for anyone, no one could possibly say, or whether beneath the hard, flippant, banal surface, the hint of lonely melancholy was real or simply another act. Beyond the few spare facts with which he had, long ago, recommended himself into our lives, we knew nothing about his past: whether it had been dull and commonplace, romantic and adventurous, blameless or criminal. No one knew. No one ever asked. To pry into the privacy of that strange soul would have been as unthinkable as spying on the dealer's hand in a good game of poker. Nor did George ever carelessly slip, face up, a card that by the rules of the game was meant to land face down. There was nothing in the ruddy, brown face, his quick, energetic step, his roar of laughter, the blatantly deceptive melancholia of his eyes to cause us to suspect that, after twenty years, any change might be taking place within him. And so the change came with an abruptness which made it all the more terrible and impossible to comprehend, even within the mystery that was George's life from the beginning to its sudden end.

He had taken Annie Chamay and my sister Hope to lunch at his favorite New York spot, Jack and Charlie's "21." He had seemed in excellent spirits, teasing Hope, who was now a lovely, delicate-looking young woman of twenty, about how the terrible racket made by her multitude of ten-cent-store bangles at the opera the evening before had drowned out the voice of the prima donna in her most climactic moment.

Suddenly in the midst of their laughter, he had risen abruptly

157

and, slapping his forehead in apparently amused consternation, had announced, "Jesus, I'm sorry, girls. You won't believe me, but I have one hell of an important date I'd completely forgotten. Look, I can't miss it. Do me a favor and pay the bill." Tossing some notes on the table, he had given each a light, affectionate kiss on the brow, turned on his heel and walked quickly out into the street. Several hours later, Beth Leary was called to identify him. He had been found lying across his bed in the Hotel St. Regis, dead of a heart attack.

At his funeral everyone gathered as if in a kind of grand finale at the closing performance of a play which everyone had thought too good to be allowed to come to an end. The New England Museum Cabinet Set was there; the Buchmanites, Great Aunt Julia and Aunt Harriet, the Countess, who had always borne a rare soft spot in her heart for George. All his old friends from Hollywood and Broadway—the world of the theater that had never forgotten him though he had given it up to become a part of our life—were there; and of course the Three Witches, and a great body of "international white trash" who had not come together in such a mass since the days of Senlis.

Added to these were a strange collection of bright young Jewish doctors and lawyers who claimed gratitude to George for having put them through college with his generous tips during long stays with the Bromfields at the Algonquin during the twenties. And finally, with a kind of pathetic wistfulness, there had appeared the Gland Types, who, in spite of his heartless abuse of them, still could only manage to look upon his departure with a sense of regret. Wickedly acid as he had been to them, he had made them, too, laugh as they never had before and now never would again. Their attitude was touching and understandable. Indeed, there was only one figure whose attitude after George's death was incomprehensible to me and that figure was my father.

I had always known my father to be a passionate, emotional,

mood-ridden man. Yet, because of these faults (if you can call them that) , he had always seemed to me as well tolerant, kindly and understanding. He had taught us himself that a grudge was no better than a slow, festering, malignant disease. And yet, when we returned to Malabar to live after George had died, there seemed to appear for the first time in my father's makeup an unexpected streak so disturbing that even now it is difficult to write of it. For all over again I feel the rage and disappointment that I felt then, and in the end I am left unhappy and puzzled.

Listening to my father, one would have thought him to have been relieved at last of a great burden. For a man who had all his life placed such a high value on laughter, it seemed suddenly as though amusement were of no importance, as if, indeed, all those special moments of laughter, the strange, delightful enchantment which had touched everything in our lives and was now so blatantly absent, had never existed at all.

With an exaggerated air of contentment he would remark, "You have no idea what a relief it is to me to have my papers in order for the first time in my life; to know where the money's going; to have someone try to *save* something." From there, noting the bad impression he had already caused, he would elaborate, "George was really hopeless. No, don't look as though you know it all, Ell—you're a child, you don't, you can't know. The intrigue that went on. Good God, he was beginning to make my life impossible."

George was not there to defend himself. Nor, as time went by, was the audience before whom my father delivered this epitaph capable of coming to his defense. Most of them had never known him. They could only consider him now as a troublesome intriguer who had attached himself to my father and ultimately became totally dependent upon him. But I for one can never forget the laughter George gave us. If he had given nothing else it would still have, all alone, outweighed mess, extravagance, intrigue; all the rest. And if there is any reason for my feeling this way, it is in the end because my father taught me, long ago, the worth of having fun.

And I remain puzzled to this day. "Perhaps," I have said to myself, "my father's strange attitude arose out of his fanatic determination to stand alone, never admitting the indispensability of anyone." I am almost certain it had something to do with the almost frightening sense of the commonplace that came into our life the moment George went out of it. It would have been difficult—no, impossible—for whoever came to fill that void to seem anything but commonplace. Sometimes I think the idea that such a void existed was unbearable to my father. He not only sought to ignore it, but to threaten it, denounce it, frighten it away.

The "paragon" of order, neatness and economy who came after George's death to type dutifully and without comment the "humus, mucus, retch and vetch" was a plump, dowdy little Englishwoman named Mrs. Rimmer, who in a manner most foreign indeed to her surroundings never did anything without authorization from the Boss. She came over from Liverpool shortly after the arrival of her son, David, who had been hired as a gardener. And, in his usual manner, my father took them in and immediately proceeded to mold them into "great characters." Unfortunately, the material was not of Hawkins caliber. The Rimmers' reaction to my father's attempt to make them witty and fabulous was one of somewhat grim amazement, which never quite left them in all the years they remained at Malabar.

My father heightened his efforts to force the Rimmers down our throats when he saw our apathy. The result in a family full of obstinate and independent people like ourselves was what might have been expected. Our greatest lament after George's death was that suddenly everything in our world was predictable. It was a novelty to which none of us—I suspect not even my father—ever really became accustomed.

Not long after her arrival at Malabar, Mrs. Rimmer began

unargumentatively to type a novel called *Mr. Smith.* It was a book written in the current popular style, which picked apart, weakness by weakness, the dull, mediocre lives of American upper-middle-class society. It was one of those books which causes one to look at all the cheerful, placid faces of upper-middle-class people one knows and think, "Can it really be possible that all these people are on the brink of suicide?" And since the subject was one with which my father was unfamiliar, the book was not only unconvincing but as drearily melodramatic as its subject.

It was most certainly the worst thing my father ever wrote and often I wonder whether, if George had been there, it would have ever been published. Certainly there would have been some terrible battles, the result of which would undoubtedly have been improvement or abandonment.

And if George had lived, might there not have been more novels recounted without messages or morals for the sake of a good story? Or is it true what Somerset Maugham tells us, that there comes a time in every writer's life when he has told his last tale?

I can't help feeling that, in the case of my father, Maugham's generality was right. One of the last excellent stories my father ever wrote was *Wild Is the River,* a highly romantic novel about New Orleans during Reconstruction. Whenever I look again through its pages, there comes to my mind the curious yet real enough picture of George and the Boss seated together in some battered relic of a once-luxurious brothel listening with eagerness to the tale of an equally battered madam who bore traces of once great elegance and beauty. Or I see them descending the steps of a poverty-stricken boardinghouse which still had an air of ghostly magnificence about it. Together as they wandered between tall, shuttered houses, beneath iron-work balustrades hung heavy with bougainvillaea and jasmine, I hear them beginning, now in hushed voices, now with an uproarious shout that startled the policeman on his watch, to unfold the story of Tom Bedloe, the Young Baroness, Aunt Tam and Seraphine.

After *Mrs. Parkington, What Became of Anna Bolton,* and *Wild Is the River,* my father's stories, *Kenny, Colorado, The Wild Country,* were, in spite of the usual disciplined form and descriptive beauty, somehow disappointing—rather like exercises written by rote, or a wonderful spice gone tasteless with age.

Years later in *From My Experience,* he wrote, "In this age fiction writing is simply a way of making a living and for my money not a very satisfactory or even self-respecting one." The remark seems pompous and rather ungrateful, coming from one who spent a quarter of a century giving so much pleasure and entertainment by practicing that very excellent art. George would indeed have raised hell over it.

But from the creation of *Wild Is the River* to the final pronouncement of this remark, my father had come a long way on a path which led away from the world of romantic invention to what is supposedly a vastly more satisfactory world, in which he wrote simply, without necessity of inventing a story, from a great existing reserve of reality and truth. Whether the goal was in the end satisfactory, as he hoped it would be, I can never say, and sometimes I think he paid for it a little too dearly along the way. But there is one thing of which I am quite certain: that somewhere, perhaps with the last pages of *Wild Is the River,* an era came to an end. It was a wonderful, adventurous and lively era, in which, next to the Boss, George had played the most important part. If this was the case, then George, with his uncanny understanding of my father, must have realized it long before any of us. And under his flippant mask of amused indifference, I would judge that the knowledge had made him in the end a troubled and lonely man.

14

The Harvest Season

Seasons pass quickly in a country world. Those who live within it, forever preoccupied with preparation for spring and then autumn, pause only now and then to look around them at the trees planted at the very beginning, the first-born calf that no one had the heart to kill even though we had no need of a bull. The next time one lifts one's eyes to these things, the trees are giving shadow in the pasture and the bull is a heavy-muscled, fiery-eyed retired tyrant.

So it was with the season of our childhood. We had come to the farm at the ages of fourteen, eleven and six. And only a few bright summers had passed, it seemed, before we were no longer little girls who could find no greater delight than that of riding home at dusk atop a hayload, or swimming in the farm pond shot with icy springs and shadowed by the willows. At the end of one of those enchanted summers, Anne and Hope were sent away to finishing school.

I think Anne was sent in the hope that parents often have, that finishing school might perform some miracle they themselves had failed to achieve. I think they hoped that, away from home, Annie might succeed in becoming more a part of the world that surrounded her. But Annie's character in its own way was as powerful as her father's. It refused to be changed by different environment, just as it had refused to be changed by threats and entreaties. Indeed, with every summer of her return from school, Annie became more withdrawn into her own strangely inaccessible world.

It was a world piled high with books and unfinished objects. There was nothing in the way of literature from *The Ancient History of the Hebrews* to Frankenstein comics that could not absorb her attention to the point of hypnosis. Wherever she went, she carried a book with her to be opened the moment an opportunity presented itself. Breakfast was her favorite meal, because seated in the kitchen with a cup of coffee perched before her she could indulge by the hour in *The Habits of the Luluaba Tribes* without being disturbed by the usual trivial mealtime conversation. No idle moment was ever wasted in bookless abandon, no matter how unwieldy her posture. I believe she could have kept on reading strung from a scaffold by her left toe. Indeed, one of my most vivid memories of my eldest sister is of her supine on an operating table, one arm outstretched, the other firmly balancing Sartre's *Being and Nothingness* before her eyes as her blood drained unheeded into a Red Cross Blood Bank receptacle.

She absorbed everything thoroughly and pondered it constantly. More than one stranger at the Bromfield dining table sweated and fidgeted under her baleful, unmoving stare, only to discover later on that, as she studied the freckle on his left cheek, she had had nothing more or less on her mind than Jung's conception of the human race.

It was that same all-inclusive imagination that created the unfinished objects: friezes of cardboard decorated with bizarre and fantastic designs of colored paper cut from magazines, and clay madonnas molded from the saffron and gray earth of Switzer's Creek. Sometimes too, in the jumble of the big room above the dairy that had been given her as a studio, one of us would come upon a few lines of poetry of vivid and haunting splendor that would trouble us for days afterward. "Why? Why did Annie never finish anything?"

The Boss called the studio "Collyer's Mansion," and he and Annie often laughed together over its chronic state of upheaval. But often too I know that both of them were deeply troubled by that ingredient strangely absent from Annie's makeup that kept all the brilliance and beauty of her nature as inaccessible as a magnificent, tangled forest in which man is unable to walk.

Time and again my parents tried to find a way to help Annie put her immense knowledge and power of reasoning to practical use; and establish a relationship with the everyday world of which she, as all of us, had to be a part. But the manner that had been her own since she was born was not to be changed. And so she remained, loneliest when among us, happiest when alone, walking in the woods or along Switzer's Creek. Her knowledge and intelligence remained like unsown seed, wasted because they could not return their fruits to earth. No one realized this better than my father. But it was one of the frustrations which now amused, now infuriated him, that he was powerless to defeat.

Of the three of us, Hope always provided him with the greatest pleasure, the least cause for concern. Indeed, only occasional refreshing outbursts of Bromfield hysterics and stubbornness saved her from being what Jane Austen would have described as "a perfectly charming and talented young lady." She wrote, drew and painted well, and sang and played the piano with a warmth, vigor and emotion that made her elders long with melancholy for their youth. Her homecoming was always a moment of eager excitement for the Boss. And, as they danced together in the hall, whirling lightly and expertly to the waltz from *Aurora's Wedding*, it was easy to see in his eyes the same pleasure and pride that had shone long ago when together they sped down Mt. Cellerina in Switzerland. She grew up sensitive, beautiful and elegant. The stubborn streak remained, beneath the beauty, and this will of iron was a source of comfort to my father. Even when she defied him, which she often did, I believe his final feeling was one of triumph. For he wanted her to be strong, to know what she wanted from life.

Certainly she shared the same intense sensitivity, telling her what was real and what was false, what was worth while and what was not. Like the Boss, she was always a straight thinker. And, like the Boss, she was, oddly enough, never ruthless. To describe the two of them it would be necessary to use an old-fashioned term. They were valiant. When they saw their star, whatever the opinion of others they never abandoned it. They were very much alike; and Hope has not changed to this day.

I, the youngest daughter, somehow escaped being sent off to boarding school. Perhaps the fact that my parents were not two, but four—my mother, father, Nanny and George—saved me from exile during my formative years. They were characters so diverse that during all the years together they could never even agree immediately on such weighty problems as whether to serve the salmon with yellow or green mayonnaise. Imagine then the complexity of deciding what to do about the education of a child. I actually believe that by the time I was old enough for my education to be planned for a kind of apathy had set in over all of them.

As a result, I became the product of a progressive American public school education, upon which my strong but generally unconstructive willfulness thrived. Now, years later, I find myself awakening to the wonders of art, literature, music and philosophy that have surrounded me always. While in high school, I learned little more than how to wear my hair shamelessly in pincurls in public. Certainly my behavior contributed more than anything else to my father's growing conviction that all children should be locked in a deep freeze from the age of twelve until they are old enough to vote. During those years, our father ignored us as best he could. And when he turned to look at us again, we were young women, inherently obstinate, independent, eager, defiant, seeking lives of our own.

He had sworn often and loudly that, once he'd gotten rid of us, he would begin life all over again and live exactly as he pleased. When I was eighteen and Hope was twenty-four, we suddenly gave him the opportunity to do just that by marrying within two weeks of one another.

Hope's wedding to a tall, gentle, strongly determined New Englander named Bob Stevens was, like The Salon in the Presbytère, touched with the kind of elegance, wealth and grandeur of which our father had always unadmittedly dreamed. He had never quite gotten over his boyhood wonder at the great and fashionable people of the world. It still excited him deeply to be ranked among them. And so, when Hope married into the old and highly connected family of J. P. Stevens, he called it the "Marriage of Two Great Worlds." From time to time, during the unwrapping of an incredible influx of wedding gifts, as one of his boxers arose, snorting and wriggling from beneath a great white drift of wrapping paper, he would take the dog's head between his hands and sigh with mock weariness, "It's a hell of a thing, Prince, old boy, but that's what comes of being famous and knowing so many people." He was happily triumphant; touchingly reassured. For here, after all, was proof again of the faith of an ambitious small-town boy who, by his own force, doing what he loved best to do, had achieved in his life all that he had set out to achieve.

He planned the wedding all himself, ordering the right food and wines, filling the house with gay, natural bouquets of flowers that bore robustness and life and none of the stiffness of those by a florist who makes funeral wreaths and wedding bouquets alike—deadly. And on the day of the wedding, as he gave away his daughter in the great front hall and Miss Hotzenpfeffer, the organist from the Episcopal Church, boomed out Lohengrin's

Wedding March on the grand piano, seven boxers came thundering enthusiastically out of the bedroom where they had been outrageously confined, virtually knocking bridegroom, father and pastor off their feet. Then, while the guests gaily celebrated, the bride and groom, dressed in parkas and ski pants, disappeared in a driving blizzard for a honeymoon in the Rocky Mountains under fifteen feet of snow. It was all, indeed, exactly as a Bromfield wedding should have been.

My wedding, two weeks afterward in the Little Church Around the Corner, New York, was as well the marriage of two worlds. But worlds which, each delightful in themselves, came together as often as gefüllte fish and caviar.

Carson and I had met the year before at Cornell, where both of us were studying agriculture. That Carson, born and raised in the heart of Brooklyn, should want to study agriculture immediately aroused my father's suspicions. He forgot that once long ago he had made up his own mind to leave the farm and go to New York to be a writer. What he did remember was the atmosphere he had encountered when he reached that great city —the atmosphere into which Carson was born.

He had glimpsed it first in the theatrical world with which, in his early life as a theater critic, he had come in contact daily. He held in his mind a memory of quick, hard-driving, often obnoxious young writers, agents and advertising men with grating Brooklyn accents, and overly disturbed feelings about social injustice. The picture didn't seem to suit Carson, but neither did the atmosphere of morning chores and long hot days in the field. How could anyone who had come from the mole-tunnel atmosphere of the New York subway want to be a farmer? My father rapidly concluded that Carson had chosen the profession because he thought there was some easy trick to it.

Unfortunately, several incidents during the summer of our courtship at Malabar Farm hastened to add weight to his theory. The first occurred on the fateful evening when, backing the

Boss's new station wagon out of the garage, Carson failed to notice that the car door was open. With a grinding of steel and a crumbling of mortar, he managed in one efficient action to remove both the car door and a post whose primary function was to support the room above it. It was an added misfortune that the room was, at that time, occupied by the stalwart and dedicated Mrs. Rimmer. Her "lummes and blimeys," as she leaned out the window suspended over nothingness, rent the night air with even greater impact than the sound of the crash, causing my father, who had been serenely hosing tomatoes on the lawn, to come charging onto the scene wild-eyed and brandishing a butcher knife.

With the agility of his old football days, Carson managed to avoid my father's indiscriminate swings, thus sparing himself for an act on the following afternoon that was even more convincing. The Boss had just begun one of his mowing excursions on the lower forty acres when he looked up to see his future son-in-law determinedly drive a jeep into the back of a stationary wagon loaded with hay.

Later on, his eyes flashing fire at the recollection of his only jeep prostrate beneath a ton of baled hay, he was heard to groan again and again, "Jesus Christ, it's a psychopathic urge to destroy!" The conviction grew and fed on itself like a disease, so that ever afterward my father was unable to approach Carson without first circling him cautiously the way one does the irresponsible hind legs of a horse. Nor would his faith in Carson begin to stir until, a long time afterward, he met him again on his own ground in another world, far removed from Malabar Farm.

In the meantime, after the wedding, while Carson served his term in the Army, I went to live alone in the Rose house, the neat white cottage where Max Drake had lived as farm manager in the beginning. It was already deeply familiar to me because of the hours I had spent long ago beneath its slanting roof, dozing in a chair while the "planning" went on into the early hours of the morning. It was shaded by the largest elm in Richland County, from whose roots a spring flowed, forming a pond beneath the kitchen window. The tree lent an air of great permanence and shelter and the house itself had the dignity of an old farmhouse, simply, solidly and honestly built. While I lived in it, I knew the very special peace and happiness which only that kind of house is capable of providing. It is the kind of house I hope, one day, I shall be fortunate enough to live in for the rest of my life.

Hope and Bob bought the Douglas Farm, a stretch of fertile field and forest that joined Malabar where the high hills braced by sandstone cliffs gave way to a deep green valley of alfalfa and brome and ladino clover where the milk cattle were loosed in the last days of August. Switzer's Creek ran through the two farms and, once again, as we had not done in many years, we found ourselves walking together with our father along the stream, gathering wild flowers, watching the dogs leap high above the growing wheat as we looked over the land.

In the evening, we often returned to Bob and Hope's comfortable farmhouse to sit by the hour planning and talking crops. With a Scotch and soda in his hand, the Boss would lean back in an armchair, regard Bob with the look of an old man who has been through it all and is willing to bestow, with great generosity, his vast, accumulated knowledge upon the eager, hard-working, intelligent *upstart*. Bob, in return, would eye the Boss with a mingling of defiance, suspicion and awe.

For all his lordliness, the Boss was as ever instinctively shy in the presence of the family. There was that dual horror of intimacy and disapproval which always caused him to begin his conversations with us by assault.

"What in hell are you building down there with that road scraper, a goddamn Arc de Triomphe?"

Fire would flicker immediately in Bob's generally calm blue eyes. "Just a cattle trail to take the steers to the back pasture. Might as well do it the *right* way the first time."

"Cattle trail!" My father never lost an opportunity to dig at what he considered Bob's conflicting extravagances and New England miserliness. "Good Christ, you could take a cordon of tanks through there and still have room for your *ten* steers!" Then, his wrinkle-scarred face lighting with inventiveness, he would add, "But while you're at it, why don't you build a couple of farm ponds? It's easy enough; if you like, I'll make you a plan—that lower hayfield there where the drainage is bad would be perfect."

One could see the disappointment come into the Boss's eyes as, leaning forward eagerly and perhaps a bit aggressively, Bob would answer, "I *have* a plan. I was thinking of just that spot, planting it with willow and sodding it in with bluegrass."

"Bluegrass!" The Boss's big frame almost twisted and turned with agony, wrinkles giving birth to wrinkles on a face grown so pliant with the years that it was capable of three or four expressions within the space of a minute. "That noxious weed? You must be out of your mind!"

And so the conversation would carry on, often through supper and into the night, bearing in it the first real hope of realizing the dream of continuation our father had begun long ago and, at the same time, the seeds of that dream's destruction.

For our father had achieved what every farmer hopes for. His daughters had married men who knew and loved and wanted, more than anything else, to care for the land. And yet, now that this continuation, for which the Boss himself had longed in the beginning, was almost certainly assured, there seemed to hang over it all a sense of doubt and regret which sometimes burst out with the noisy apprehension of a trapped wild elephant.

Unconsciously, Carson and I increased this apprehension by searching within the world of Pleasant Valley for a farm of our own. It would not have been difficult to find. How often we came upon "the place," and as Carson looked over the fields, I stood on a weathered porch looking out over a ruined garden, thinking of how it would all be.

Like Hope and Bob, we had chosen Pleasant Valley primarily because it was to us one of the most satisfyingly beautiful and worth-while places to live in the world. But at the same time, independent, on land of our own, we hoped that we might be near by to give the help which, more and more as time went on, it became obvious that my father needed.

Much as he liked to consider himself proficient in all trades, the Boss was no good at a bargain. He probably would have been able to design logical economic patterns for the world which, put into competent hands, would easily have had success. But to sit down and figure out when to sell the hogs and how much to take on an old tractor was somehow not within his grasp. Typical of his business transactions was the deal he made in the sale of an old silo by which he ended up paying the purchaser twice the selling price to haul it away.

Someone with the time and concern for everyday practicalities, someone with less vision, perhaps, but more patience, could have given him the help he needed when, already overburdened with speech commitments and the details of the farm, he had less and less time to devote to his own source of income: writing.

He was, like every American farmer, caught up in the economic chaos caused by price supports and government controls, plus heavy taxes on the proceeds from his books. At the same time, he was committed to a farming program that reaped material benefits for others but seldom for himself. Once he had proved some new method satisfactorily, he would begin something new in the interest of agricultural development. His satisfaction with new ideas and his delight in making them actually work never gave him time to gain the profit of a single steady program.

Nor would he, in any way, concede to the idea of living in a more modest fashion. As long as he lived in it, the Big House was never silent and empty, his table was always as abundantly heaped with good food and drink and alive with the talk and laughter of a great many people as it had been from the beginning.

And yet, each year the expenses grew greater and greater and the means to pay them less. We were young and new and naïve in farming and none of us were financial geniuses. But I can't help feeling even now that, had he put his trust in us, had we all worked together, our farms and Malabar would have accomplished the continuation and permanence he had envisioned with such eagerness at the beginning and he would not, at the end of his life, have been such a lonely and defeated man.

But not only had he always been incapable of delegating responsibility; the truth was that he didn't believe in us. I can imagine how on sleepless nights his thoughts whirled around in his head while in the darkness the dogs rushed in and out of all those doors of his, barking with the nervous restlessness he had instilled in every cranny of the room. All those years of work to make the farm the special thing it was. He was not about to change it for a lot of upstarts. And how could we understand it as he did? Hope and I, who, under the corrosive influence of George, had defiantly refused to listen to a Sunday speech or ever go on a farm tour. Somehow, during those restless, thought-filled nights, it became clear to my father that accepting our help in any way would upset the balance of his life.

We had too many ideas and, good or bad, they didn't suit him. In the back of his mind I believe the thought ran that there was not really room at Malabar for ideas that were not his own. The thing was too precious to him, too much an expression of himself, to risk its sharing. Indeed, in his heart of hearts, he could not have borne to share it with anyone else.

One could not rightly dispute so deeply felt a conviction. And, in any case, had we ever proved ourselves worthy of offering our assistance? Sometimes such proof only comes when it can no longer be of any use and, since there is no way of ripening a thing before its time, there is nothing to do but sit back and watch the time slip away.

15

Time to Go

In theory, my father, having rid his household of two obstinate, self-willed daughters, was living at last as he liked. Actually, he knew as well as we did that he had never lived otherwise. The people who surrounded him daily were there at his invitation. Those who avoided him did so because they dared not do otherwise. The divergence of characters, the intrigue and chaos that sometimes reached the magnitude of Louis XV's court, existed because he had never been able to avoid becoming entangled in the lives of those who caught his imagination.

Among those who had deftly caught and held his imagination from the very beginning was Nanny. She had always been more to us than simply a governess. She had been a part of our lives, outwardly strict and conscious of position at the most frustrating times and places. Inwardly she was game for anything from wearing out the derrierè of her sensible skirt sliding down the dunes at Ermenonville, to joining the Boss and George in an outing to the Folies Bergéres.

As she grew older, her energies, rather than diminish, seemed to increase so that at Malabar Farm, rather than rest on her laurels now that the youngest child was potty trained, she found every reason possible to multiply her duties. It was Nanny who planted the first vegetable garden and brought corn and sweet peas steaming hot and dripping with butter to the table. The first flowers and bushes that surrounded the ugly mail-order house took root under her expert gardener's hands. In mid-summer, when the wild grapes and chokecherries began to turn black on the trees and vines along the dusty country roads, she led us on long berrying expeditions into the wild country. And, late at night, trusting no one with her hard-won harvest, she strained and boiled the berries into wonderful tart jams and jellies.

She had been brought up by dour Scots who believed that a hard bench in a cold, damp church brought one closer to God. And although reason and a sense of humor had taught her early the trick of concealing a pack of cards in her Bible, nevertheless she absorbed in her youth a lifelong conviction that achievement came only through suffering.

Everything had to be done the hard way. Laundry had to be boiled, thrice washed, twice rinsed and starched according to a formula so complicated that it was unfathomable to anyone but herself. With time, the cook learned to stand aside while she did the canning; and a long series of butlers discovered it was more practical to read the funnies and listen to the baseball game while Miss White did the dishes than try to master the fantastically complicated ritual Nanny found necessary for the production of a sterile dish. In the end, everyone learned that it was better not to try to obstruct Nanny's fanatic pursuit of exhaustion. And indeed she seldom encountered any sizable obstacle unless, as was inevitable, her path crossed that of the Boss.

Then the sparks flew. Melodramatic exhibitions ensued such as the one which occurred when, one Sunday in the heat of midsummer, my father decided to serve cold salmon rather than the usual chicken for lunch. With great care, he prepared the fish and left it, delicately seasoned and cooked to a delectable pink, in the icebox overnight.

In the morning, Nanny descended to the kitchen, sniffed the salmon suspiciously and decided it wasn't cooked enough. "I'll just pop it in the oven for another hour and he'll never know the difference," she confided to me with a conspiratorial air that seemed to have gained in self-justification with the years.

The result was a fish that had turned from a tender pink to the color and consistency of salt cod. Its appearance on the buffet, served with yellow mayonnaise at a time when the Boss was in favor of green, brought an apoplectic roar of curses and martyred shrieks which terminated in a moment's awed silence after Annie, in Nanny's defense, struck her father on the head with a serving spoon.

The incident was remembered ever afterward as "the warm salmon scene." But, often as the Boss threatened to re-enact it in all its terribleness, Nanny continued life in the usual manner, unperturbed. Probably this was because she knew it was always the Boss who got struck with the serving spoon and not herself. The Boss would begin a tirade, rallying us all to her side, no matter how justifiable his rantings were. It was simple enough. Somewhere in the dark nights when she had rocked us to sleep and the rainy days when she had entranced us by turning an entire nursery into a spider's web by tying strings to lamps and door-knobs, she had become omnipotent to us.

Nanny could do no wrong. Not even when the Boss suggested a simple picnic of hot dogs and roasted corn on Mt. Jeez and she managed to expand his plans so that an extra wagon was needed to transport four different salads, roast meats, cakes and pies and plates enough for a ten-course banquet. Indeed, all my memories of picnics on Mt. Jeez proceed with the vision of my father driving the tractor with the determination of Ben Hur; while in the wagon behind Nanny sat on a bale, clutching a sloshing, splashing bowl of fruit punch and lecturing interminably above the tractor's roar. "You'd think there was nothing to it. Hot dogs indeed. Horrid indigestible things. He never thinks of my gas. I'd like to see what would happen if once I did what he told me."

This last possibility, tossed threateningly into the wind, was one that in all their twenty-six years together was never realized. She might have gone on forever, obstinate, comic and beloved, had not life at Malabar itself begun to change.

I suppose the first real change began with George's death. For not only did my father lose his greatest friend and critic, but Nanny as well seemed to have suffered an irreparable loss. Gone was the disrespectful, unpredictable madman who had once challenged her to a footrace in tennis shoes from Malabar to Mansfield. Gone was the co-conspirator who managed to cover the fact that Hope had been overcharged at Halles; or, when necessity called, diverted funds from the purchase of chicken feed to new curtains for the living room; or, in loud whispers behind closed doors, managed to solve half the problems of the household before they ever came to the Boss's attention.

In George's place, with the hell-bent gait of a chicken crossing the road before a two-ton truck, came the new secretary, Mrs. Rimmer, to straighten out my father's affairs. Her unreasonable efficiency and an annoying tendency to take the Boss at his word in a household where confusion and obstinacy had become a kind of religion were difficult for Nanny to bear. Added to that, Mrs. Rimmer had that Cockney accent. Nanny managed to bear it for five years, though her King's English became more pronounced with every "luv" and "coo" that Mrs. Rimmer uttered. Then, a few months after Hope and I were safely raised and married, she packed up her belongings and, for the first time without a suitable retort to my father's incredulous questioning look, she went to live with Hope at the Douglas farm.

The Boss heaved an appropriate sigh of relief and repeated the somewhat stale pronouncement that now at last he would live as he liked. Perhaps so. Yet when we climbed the hill to visit the

Big House no one could deny that something was gone; something of zeal, obstinacy and comic confusion. But, most of all, something of devotion. When the Boss laughed, he laughed loud, but not so often and sometimes with a lack of conviction, that led us to believe that he was living less as he liked every day.

It was during the time that Bob and Hope and Nanny still lived nearby on the Douglas Farm and Carson and I still searched hopefully for a place nearby that my mother's illness became worse. Her heart had been weak ever since she had contracted rheumatic fever as a child. It was a weakness which, with time, came to limit her every action and to cause her to withdraw more and more into a world of helplessness and defeat. Not everyone is thus affected by a heart condition. But a great deal depends upon ambition, a tough spirit, necessity. My mother's one ambition had been to please my father, and since such an idea was from the beginning a disconcerting one to him, she never succeeded. Could she have cloaked that frail heart with some of the toughness of her little Aunt Julia, things might have been different. But she couldn't, and though she never quite admitted defeat, still her life became a gradual but continuous retreat.

Her smile became more fixed. Her conversation, once so charmingly candid, became cautiously banal, for she lived in terror of saying the wrong thing and causing a scene. She was, more than ever, a pathetic, ghostly figure, lost in a world of vigorous, ambitious, busy people who never understood what it was to be helpless. In the end, I believe, helplessness became her true illness and, defeated by it, she retired to the quiet room that for all still seemed filled with special light.

We visited her there with dutiful deference, taking time out from our busy lives, each minute of which, to us, seemed infinitely precious. Of all of us, I believe only Anne understood that in a sense our time was not important at all. Anne seldom left her mother's side.

Most of the time, she sat on the now faded pink chaise longue, surrounded by heaps of paper and the three or four books she was currently reading, immersed in Greek mythology or scribbling a poem or just staring at some inanimate object—thinking. If she spoke at all, it was more often than not in answer to some parenthetical question she had been silently pondering. As a result, her mother would be awakened in the midst of a doze by a rather strident voice which boomed assertingly, "No! I can't think it possible that the Greeks could have believed all that rot. They must have used it to keep the other damn fools in order. But I'll hand it to them, their imaginations were incredible."

My mother, seeing that no response was necessary, would close her eyes again or perhaps take up a novel and begin to read. She had even given up fretting over Anne's strange ways. And in accepting them I think she found a certain peace. Theirs was an odd companionship, and yet, to my mother, it must have been in its way comforting; for shy, reserved, absorbed in her thoughts as she was, I believe Anne could understand better than any of us the dreadfulness of being alone.

And so it was Anne who found our mother on the morning of her death. As she came out of the room, just now being lit by that familiar soft sunlight, I was the first person she encountered. She stood in the doorway and spoke in an odd, constrained voice. "Mummy is dead," she said simply and her face depicted at once all the things that made her as she was: the deep, calm cognizance of the ways of life and at the same time the shock and incredulity of a child.

I hope our mother died in peace, with one of Anne's rare, good-hearted truths firmly implanted in the back of her mind. None of us can ever know. It all seemed to happen so suddenly and yet, of course, it hadn't. The only thing that really made it seem that way was that, in all the years since our birth, none of us children had ever really taken the time to know her. And something tells me that, in his horror of sentimentality, this was true of the Boss as well.

I still cannot tell what it was that gave that special atmosphere of peace and sunlight to her room. I only know that after she died and they took away her bed and most of her special private possessions and made her room into a guest room, the atmosphere was gone. It became like any other room. And not only that. We soon discovered that, without our knowing, that strange, quiet pleasantness had existed beyond the room in every part of the house and now was suddenly gone. In its place came a kind of emptiness, sad, a certain lack of grace, which could never be replaced. It was odd. Though my mother had scarcely ever done more than arrange the flowers or fix my father a drink as the light faded, there was now a barrenness: something hard and comfortless, as if a woman of great dignity and warmth and knowledge had gone from the house.

Though my father, in a characteristic way, never openly acknowledged the strange emptiness, it would have been impossible for him not to have sensed it as well. That he obviously couldn't forget it became clear several years after her death, when he built on the Nimen Place, before an old spring house where we had often quenched our thirst, a vegetable stand with great tanks through which the spring water flowed, fountainlike, over and about the vegetables, keeping them cool and fresh in the dead heat of summer. The vegetable stand became a gathering place where Sunday drivers stopped to buy the fine, fresh produce from the garden and to stand around and talk beneath the shadow of old trees and hear the cool sound of those constantly flowing waters.

At one side of the stand, which was built of sandstone from the surrounding countryside, my father placed a plaque with the inscription: "To the memory of Mary Appleton Bromfield, who also loved this valley and found here peace, happiness and abundance."

The Heritage

How often I have wished that he had had the strength of heart in this case to make some such tribute when my mother could have been there to read it. Perhaps then the words would have held less of a sense of wistful emptiness and regret.

After my mother's death, as before, I climbed the hill often to visit my father, and occasionally he came to have dinner with me in the kitchen of the Rose cottage at the bottom of the hill. Sometimes he brought along an old friend; sometimes he brought along a stranger, perhaps a Brazilian, who had read his books and was filled with an intense enthusiasm for creating a Malabar Farm on Brazilian soil. In either case, with the friend who was intelligent and delightful company, or the stranger who was awed and fascinated, the evening passed happily. In the relieving atmosphere of performing before an audience, we joked easily, argued, exchanged ideas as friends. It was as we both longed for it to be and I still maintain that the moments of "putting on an act" had a far greater ring of our real feelings than those ghastly moments when we found ourselves alone. Then the fact that we were father and daughter seemed to rise up between us in an impenetrable wall of panic.

We remembered then that we were "at odds" over the running of the farm; that deeply, inexplicably, without our intending it, rather than bring us together the land we both loved had come between us. We longed to span this ridiculous barrier, to clarify and to assure one another. But on this point perhaps we were too much alike: too stubborn, too shy and fearful of a show of sentimentality to be able to find a basis on which to begin. We circled, talked uncomfortably of nothing, and as soon as possible, my father, pleading "mountains of work," excused himself and went away.

More and more often as I sat alone at dusk, looking over the land I knew and loved perhaps more than any land before or after, I was struck with the sensation that I was saying good-by. It was obvious that the Boss, as long as he could walk, talk, think and act in his noisy, expansive way, could never share his valley. Whatever the price of remaining alone and independent, he would gladly pay it. Then, too, perhaps the brilliant light he had cast over that valley gave his children little room in which to cast lights of their own. It was almost as if by some unspoken mutual consent we owned that it was time to go.

Not long after Carson finished his stay in the Army, we boarded a ship in New Orleans and headed for Brazil. And a month later, Hope and Bob sold the Douglas Farm on Switzer's Creek and moved to Virginia to begin all over again on a new piece of land, leaving the Boss alone.

 # 16

The White Room

My father had been to Brazil before us. He had traveled over the coffee lands of Paraná by jeep and muleback. He had flown with Moura Andrade, the Brazilian cattle king, over the forests and campo and swamps of the Great Pantanal and in São Paulo had roamed over the fazendas of Lunardelli, the brilliant old Italian peasant who had created fortunes and coffee empires wherever new land was opened. He had been received in the literary salons of São Paulo and Rio and, visiting fazendas in the vast interior, had spoken to many a fazendeiro about the land.

He liked the Brazilians for the strange combination in their natures of expansiveness and pessimism, born of life in a country where each step toward development encountered untold difficulties. He liked them for their intense pride, their great good humor, their individuality, which somehow so delightfully frustrated most attempts at serious organization.

He loved and understood Brazil almost immediately, as if, indeed, he had known it all his life. Out of his enthusiasm for this huge, rich, disorganized country and the other lands of the Western Hemisphere that surrounded it, he wrote a book called *A New Pattern for a Tired World*. The book is based on his belief that the development of an economically strong and united Western Hemisphere is not only necessary for the survival of its own democracy and civilization, but is the greatest and perhaps the only hope for the survival of democracy and civilization in the entire world. It is a sound book and goes to all lengths to save what is worth saving. It was formed in a mind which, in spite of everything, never lost its common sense nor its humor, nor its continuous dynamic capacity for thinking big.

Even before *A New Pattern for a Tired World* was published, there were already a great many Brazilian fazendeiros who felt that the influence of my father's agricultural knowledge would do a great deal to further the practice of soil conservation and the transition from monoculture to general agriculture in the many regions of Brazil where the latter could be successfully practiced. It was for this reason that a group of Brazilians, with Manöel Carlos Aranha, one of São Paulo's finest farmers, as their leader, formed Fazenda Malabar-do-Brasil.

The fazenda lay in the valley of the River Atibaia, a broad lowland which ended abruptly in steep jagged hills that were almost mountains, covered with pink and gray granite boulders and dense, tangled forests. And it was here that Carson and I and our small son, Steve, after several uncertain months in Brazil, went to work and live.

A hundred years ago, the valley of the Atibaia had been rich and prosperous, in a time when slaves had cleared the forests and planted coffee, even amongst the boulders that were scattered over the summits of those jagged serras. But with time the slaves had been freed, the soils depleted, and the fazenda abandoned to become covered with second-growth forest, broom grass and the long, tangled vines of bright orange St. John's flower.

By the time we came to it, the valley had much in common with those old run-down farms my grandfather and father had tried to salvage long ago. Only this was a summer country, in which the growth was lush and tropical the year round. For the first six months Carson worked almost entirely at trying to clear the weeds.

He worked with tractors and with men and mules who came in after the tractors had bulldozed and plowed away the brush, to open the furrows and plant the first seed. Most of the men were Brazilians who had become accustomed to living on a farm that had lost its purpose. Their forebears had planted coffee; and when the coffee had been abandoned, they had remained to herd the half-wild cattle that wandered at will among the termite hills and weeds. Such had been their existence and their fathers' existence for the better part of a hundred years. The surge of activity at Fazenda Malabar was something of a shock — especially to those who had not even been told that the fazenda had been sold — but those who survived the shock and remained worked hard and well.

They worked together with Italian immigrants — the tenders of vineyards from the mountain country round Milan, who had come to stake a new claim and begin a new life on Brazilian soil. Argumentative, dramatic, energetic, ambitious, the Italians carried on the whole drama of love, hate, sorrow and laughter as they worked in the fields. And often at night from the "colonia dos trabalhadores" across the way, we would hear lifted above the sounds of night in the country a clear, strong and beautiful voice singing a Puccini aria. Half the time those Italians did not know what they were singing, but only that the song was their birthright. It sounded strange in the midst of the half-wild Brazilian country, but it was a sound that would in time become familiar: the voices of new people come to fill a great, empty land.

In Fazenda Malabar's beginning, there came all manner of men. Japanese came and with their great endurance and determination cleared the swamps and put the black earth to producing strawberries, cabbages and lettuce. A young deposed Spanish marquis joined us, and a fortune seeker from California. Most of us spoke some language that none of the others understood. We were

186

short of funds and short of experience. But there was something that bound us all together in a manner that is shared by people only when they have a real challenge to face.

We all had a tremendous pride and love for that run-down, improbable fazenda. The very hardships — the drought, flood, disease, a frost that overnight destroyed the work of a year — served to intensify our feelings. We were determined to make the fazenda succeed.

And, in the end, it did succeed. The fazenda produced, and a great many families lived well and proudly from the land. It was our hardest and happiest experience in working for others. It taught us in the very beginning things about the Brazilian people and their earth that would be invaluable to us for the rest of our lives.

The house in which we lived was reminiscent of the Presbytère de St. Etienne, for it, too, with its thick clay walls and low tile roof, was old and crumbling, yet somehow indestructible. It stood not far from the river, shaded by two immense kapok trees and bound to earth by masses of flowering vines so that it gave the impression of having grown out of the very earth on which it stood.

I think my father felt relief the moment he saw it: relief at its solidness and peacefulness, relief at its age and a certain clean earthiness. And I think he was immensely relieved to see that we loved the old house, understood the value of its decrepit solidity, which made one feel so at peace, so at home.

His pleasure at our understanding was something which began warily and grew with caution during the days we spent together on the fazenda. It had been over a year since we had seen him and since he had discovered, with horrow and even a sense of having been double-crossed, that Carlito Arañha had chosen us for the job of running the fazenda. During that time, the Boss must have suffered agonies of anxiety which expressed themselves in discouraging letters full of reprimands such as these:

The Heritage

I'll tell you frankly, I was appalled when I discovered that Carlito had chosen you for the job. From experience, Ellen, I know that you are willful and stubborn like your aunt Marie. In your desire to have your way — do as you please — you have a way of rudely stepping on the people who try to help you. This won't do with the Brazilians. They are an extremely intelligent, tactful and well-educated people. When I think of you with your lack of experience and education, Christ, my blood runs cold. But there is nothing to do but make the best of it. . . .

In answer to our suggestion that his use of "Don" in one of his Brazilian books, in reference to Carson, was perhaps an exaggeration, we received the following wildly contradictory tirade:

As to the problem (?) of the use of Don or Dona you — Mr. Geld — still have a lot to learn. Rio is filled with Dons and Donas. Anybody can be a "Doctor" in Brazil. "Don" is essentially a title of rank and of achievement. All the Braganza family (deposed royalty) are entitled to be addressed as Don or Dona. It is a much more distinguished title than that of "Doctor," which indeed is hooked on to anyone who has been through the third grade. Where have you been all this time? As a matter of fact, the one time I ever answered the phone in Brazil the call was for Dona *Elena.*

We might have responded that nevertheless, unflattering as it might seem, Carson was referred to as "Doutor." We could as well have added that Dona is a title used for every housewife in Brazil and that in our admittedly scant two years in this country we had never heard the title Dom, as it is spelled in Portuguese, applied to anyone but a Bishop. Though as yet, living in out-of-the-way Itatiba as we did, we were not acquainted with the Bragança family. But at the time the energy that would have required made it seem better to just let him rant.

Still, when at last he did come to the fazenda and we walked

188

out over the land together, through the rice which stood waist high, bending with the weight of its grain, his worst suspicions seemed at last to leave him. Wariness began to give way and a great ease and friendliness grew in its place. It was almost as if the terrible shyness and suspicion which had arisen from our being father and daughter had at last disappeared, as if now we saw one another simply as friends.

Part of the change, of course, had to do with the fact that Carson and I now lived in Brazil some six thousand miles from Malabar Farm, and apparently intended to stay. But another part arose from the discovery that we *did* see in our new life the value of many things that were of the utmost importance to him. Proof of it was indeed our love of the valley of the Atibaia, and our slowly but surely increasing understanding of the Brazilians: some of a new and rapidly growing middle class, some of old patriarchal families dating back to the days of the masters and the slaves, who came to sit on our veranda in the long, cool Brazilian twilight to drink coffee and talk endlessly and enthusiastically about the future.

"This is a new country in a different climate," he used to say to us, when at last our visitors had departed. "Look at it as such, think of it as such. Don't ever try to make things over on an American model. That's where most of these fools fail. Think of it as something almost unspoiled, with enormous possibilities. Why, just look at this fazenda. I wonder if anywhere else on earth you can grow anything from coffee to grapes to asparagus on the same land and plant four crops a year."

"But don't try to do it all yourselves in your own way," he would add with some of his old apprehension. "Listen to these people who come here; they have great experience, most of them are highly educated and certainly they're sharp and intelligent. They can help you. Earn their respect, get to know them. Re-member — *you* are the foreigner. It's incredible but I know a great

189

many Americans, Englishmen, Germans, also, who still think it's the other way around." And he would add offhandedly, "But surprisingly enough you seem to be somewhat aware of all that."

This double-edged compliment filled me with perhaps more pride than he knew, or even than it merited. As for himself, I know that, in this distant place, he found what was by then perhaps the only real peace that existed in his life. Every man needs to be alone at some time or other, and the solitude my father found at Fazenda Malabar, a solitude surrounded by the activity of the farm, which he could observe but in which he needed take no part, was a great comfort to him. It gave him the time that was rarely, if ever, permitted him in his hectic life at home, to simply remain quiet and think.

His room was at the back of the old, rambling country house, and from its windows, beneath the low, sloping eaves, he could look out upon a flamboyant tree bright with flowers in season and filled with canaries and humming birds and soft, timorous doves. Beyond lay the orchard full of tropical fruits and the calm, ponderously winding Atibaia River. All of us loved that room the best of all—perhaps for its sloping ceiling close against the roof, which during the nights of long, tropical rains gave one a quiet sense of shelter and peace.

My father wrote of it: "The walls, made of the bricks and mud that came out of the fields themselves, are whitewashed. The furniture, consisting only of a wardrobe, a bed, a single chair and a work table, is all white. There is nothing at all to distract the mind or the eye and so, within that room, there is always peace. One can think, one can read, one can write without distraction. When I am at Malabar-do-Brasil it is my room and I think I love it better than any room I have ever known."

He called it the White Room and, for it, named the last chapter of the last book he ever wrote.

The book is called, *From My Experience* and is, like the other farm books and *A New Pattern*, full of stimulating ideas, fascinating for anyone who understands or wishes to understand something of land and people and animals and plants—their relation to economics, science and the vast scheme of life itself. But it is the last chapter which catches one's attention in a different way and draws one back to read it, searchingly, again and again. For in it, cleanly and powerfully concentrated, is the story of a man's search for the meaning of living. The writer begins by telling of his discovery, as a very young man, that money is of value only when it provides freedom and experience. He goes on to tell of how, living by this conviction, he used the money he earned from his writings for travel, for acquiring knowledge through the places he came upon, the people he met, the languages he was able to learn, the books he was able to read and, not a little bit, from the life he led in the old Presbytère, in a country which he could never really call foreign but in which, from the moment of his arrival, he had felt at home.

But, after a time, he discovered that he was no longer satisfied with the way in which he was using his freedom. The continuous roaming and learning seemed somehow to lack something of which he was basically in need. All his senses were satisfied by it, and yet there persisted a growing desire to put abilities to work that had scarcely been used, to return to the land and create something with his hands that might grow and last and continue before his eyes.

So he returned to Ohio and began the creation of Malabar Farm and the Big House on the hill, with its large, friendly rooms and beautiful French furnishings, which became at once a part of the Ohio countryside he had known and loved and so often dreamed of in his long absence.

With time, his thoughts and energies became involved in what he called "the small world of the farm" almost to the exclusion of everything else. And through his work and interest in the farm there began to grow a greater and greater fascination with agriculture, science, economics and all that had to do not only with man's material, but his spiritual welfare as well.

Gradually he became convinced "that the two were not so widely and hopelessly separated as some of the more sentimental would have us believe." It began to become clear to him that for real sense, even sanity, to exist in the world, the material and the spiritual ought to be united in the lives and work of men and move together in harmony.

Still the final answer—the reason why—evaded him and continued to do so for many years, until one afternoon in the White Room of the Big House in Brazil, quite by accident, he came upon the idea he had so long sought, which after a fashion had given direction to the whole of his life.

He found it in the words of a man in most ways very different from himself, who, rather than seeking fame and position and a knowledge of a great and sophisticated world, had chosen to bury himself in a place called Lambaréné in the heart of the Belgian Congo; who, in the conviction that one must do something more than simply believe in the doctrines of Christ, had devoted his life to the black people of the forest because quite simply, he knew they were greatly in need of his help.

And so it was that while reading one afternoon in the White Room from Albert Schweitzer's *Out of My Life and Thought* my father came upon a phrase that in his own words "stimulating thought to an almost unbearable degree, illuminates the darkness like the switching on of a powerful light bulb—a phrase which is fecund and keeps breeding thought upon thought, conception upon conception."

The phrase was "a Reverence for Life." And for my father its mere conception "brought the elements of the mechanistic and the material together with the ethical and even the spiritual." "In a sense," he wrote, "it defined God for the first time, for if God is not Life, He is merely a vaporous figment of the imagination and the delusion of the weak and the frightened . . . who are so profoundly in need of help not from God so much as from their fellow men who are stronger, more intelligent, perhaps even more favored."

My father began to understand, and as I read I began at last to understand as well why he had poured out time and energy and money on things which could not possibly have provided any material return and which his family and friends had often regarded as follies. With clarity, he saw why he had never felt guilt over the commitment of what church dogma would have regarded as sin; and why, at the same time, he had never been able to practice "certain shabby things, certain cheating and short-cutting . . . without a sense of degradation."

"The real sins, the only sins," he concluded, "are those against Life itself and the principle of Reverence for Life. . . . The sin can be committed in countless ways from unkindness to the greedy ravaging of a forest, from the making of a smart deal to the wasting of land which belongs not to us but to Life and which we hold only in trust for future generations."

Indeed, my father's search had followed a very different path from that of Albert Schweitzer, one not nearly so self-sacrificing and righteous. He had often stumbled along the way.

And yet, if these two men had ever had the opportunity to meet, I believe they would have had much to talk about as people who understand one another always do. Nor would their time have been wasted. For different as they were, each of them had, as my father had written of Schweitzer, developed "all his talents and with a vigorous, robust faith not in angels and harps or purgatories or hell-fire and damnation, but in the realities of Man himself."

Each one had lived as best he could according to his principles, and each, to his own degree, would be among those lucky enough to leave, wherever he made contact with man, the notion of a way of living and thinking that was strong and illuminating; the notion of men who, indeed, before anything, lived by a Reverence for Life.

The Heritage

My father left the Valley of the Atibaia, scattering behind him volumes of plans for "pig operations," large-scale truck gardening, the mounting of a canning plant right on the fazenda. The ideas and plans continued to pour forth in letters full of enthusiasm about Brazil and amusing comments about his return trip through South and Central America. "Spanish Honduras is the rectum of the world except for the United Fruit Company Agricultural School where we lived in luxury. But I didn't see a banana or a banana plantation the whole time I was there."

At the same time, he sent me much advice and encouragement over a book I had written about our life in Brazil called *Strangers in the Valley*, which was later, in a great part due to his help in putting it in the right hands, published by Dodd, Mead.

Never in his letters was there any sign of discouragement or weariness or any word of the financial difficulties he must have been going through just trying to keep the farm in order. Nor did he mention illness until a year later, almost on the eve of his return to Brazil, when he began to mention offhandedly the discovery of "acute anemia." From Doris Duke's farm, where he stayed during part of his treatment rather than be "constantly shut up with those Goddamn infantile nurses in the hospital," he wrote.

"I'm feeling better and better. All the tests and checks have come through and are fine and the doctors have never seen a faster or more thorough recovery. I'm getting an enormous amount of work cleared up here at the Duke Farm which also makes one feel much better in the head. The doctors say I must absolutely take at least two days' rest a week from now on which I am certainly going to try to do."

What he didn't add was that the "acute anemia" was an obscure kind of cancer of the bone marrow and that, if he did not take the proper rest and cure, he would certainly die within a month.

At the most, he might have lived on for several years, an invalid with a nurse always at his side. This was the story he pledged his doctors not to give out and which actually no one discovered until a month after his return home, when, stricken with pneumonia and jaundice as well as his unspoken disease, he was taken to the Columbus Hospital.

I wrote to him three and four times a week, letters which seemed as ineffectual and empty as the great distance between us. Naturally, they were never answered. And in March, 1956, a little over a month after receiving his last letter, because of poor communications—and before the telegram which arrived over a week late—I opened the newspaper and discovered that my father had died.

17

The Heritage

Although there was no sign to tell of it, I think even a stranger arriving for the first time knew the moment he entered Malabar Farm. It happened suddenly, almost as if by enchantment, as you turned the bend in the road that led into the farm, and transported you into a world that was neither French nor American, but a little of both; and something more. It was at once romantic, earthy, garrulous and frenziedly busy, yet peaceful and beautiful as anything made by the hands of an artist who took at random hills, rivers, forests and fields and made of them a conglomeration of what he believed life itself should be.

As the Presbytère had been a reflection of my father as a young man, so was the farm the reflection of that same man grown mature and more thoughtful, more concerned with a setting down of roots and finding a reason for living beyond success. As my father grew, the farm grew with him. As he changed in his mind, the farm changed from something whose creation had been an end in itself. The Big House began to weather and bear the neglected look of something loved but forgotten in the perpetual busyness of the day. The garden on the hillside, so like the one in Senlis with its abundance and variety of carefully, personally tended plants, was taken over by periwinkle, day lilies and narcissus in season: plants that were strong enough to survive the total neglect of hands too busy discovering other things more useful, such as the best way to plant corn and legumes and fatten cattle.

Yet, as this change took place, my father never entirely gave up one life for another; never lost his love of gaiety, good food, beautiful things, or his curiosity about people. All these things gained from experience made Malabar Farm "different" from the day my father first set foot on the land to the day when suddenly, old and ill, he went away from it forever.

So, foolishly, it was still this sensation I sought when, a year after my father's death, I went back toward the farm. I had often dreamed, in the four years of our absence, of returning to Malabar; of walking over the fields and along Switzer's Creek with my father and my children at my side. In the evening, I had thought, we would sit in the big comfortable living room, listening to music, talking and laughing with the new-found ease that had come to us since our status had changed from that of father and daughter to that of friends. But now that we had at last been able to make the long trip, I would have to walk over the fields alone and, at night, return to a house whose emptiness was yet impossible for me to conceive.

On that hot July day, as we turned the bend that led into the farm, I was filled with the same elation I had so often felt coming home as a child. It was an elation I could not shake off after so many years of enchantment. It sprang up as naturally as the anticipation of seeing one you love. And then gradually, of its own accord, it seemed to die.

Beyond the multiflora rose hedge that bordered the road with its great cascades of delicate white flowers I could see the fields as they had been, heavy with beginning grain in the hot July sun. The waters of Switzer's Creek shone beneath my eyes, inviting me on a long, cool walk into the depths of the wood beyond, and in the crook of the hill I saw the Rose house under the benevolent shade of the ancient elm and my heart went out to it. And yet nothing in this scene seemed to welcome me home.

The Heritage

We turned up the road between the tall Babylonica willows and approached the Big House. It stood gray and weathered behind the greenery of hemlock and lilac and the tall walnut. But, though it was mid-July, there were no hurried comings and goings of tractors and wagons, no flurry of dogs rushing at us in joy and high excitement. For an instant, I thought the place to be entirely deserted, and then I saw one of the dogs on the lawn.

It was Rex, a big, beautiful, bounding, senseless pup when we had gone away, who had grown gray-muzzled in the four short years of our absence. He did not rush toward us with his usual exuberance, but simply sat and watched our approach, without curiosity. It was a stance I had often seen the dogs take when they knew somehow—by the size of his suitcase or the tone of guilt in his voice—that my father would be gone a long time and that the countless arrivals and departures during the interim held nothing for them. The dog was waiting and I realized that, in that hot July afternoon, suspended in stillness, the whole farm seemed to be waiting.

This sensation followed me wherever I went as, alone, I walked over the land: an emptiness that dampened every action from walking through fields of hay left to flower past their time, to wandering the wild roads where, in hot midsummer, blackberries hung fat and ripe for the picking along every wild, overgrown fencerow. Once I had gathered pecks of them. But now what would I pick them for? For whom would I make the jam the Boss had so vehemently denounced as "goddamn seed-strewn glue" and had eaten, all the same, until his teeth turned blue? I plucked a few and ate them, but their taste seemed disappointing.

In the end, I climbed to the top of Mt. Jeez to look down upon the view. But, as I reached the top at last and sprawled panting and exhausted in the soft grasses of my childhood, I saw that, rather than escape the sense of waiting, I had come here to my father's highest hill to meet it head on. I saw still below me the fields with their ribbonlike contours, the pond with its fringe of willows, the stream and the lakes that shone distant and peaceful among the forested hills. I looked over it all and I was touched with an odd sense of fragility, as if already that truce between one man and his land had come to an apathetic halt.

As if to emphasize the truth of this, as I looked across the valley toward the forest we had loved and respected for its inviolability from the very beginning, I saw, barely discernible in the distance, a strip of brown which ran from the Ferguson Place, cutting down through the forest to Switzer's Creek. But for the brown of deadness, like a scar admidst the lush green of summer, one would not have noticed the strip at all. But I knew what it was. I knew simply that it marked the beginning of the destruction of the indomitable, timeless world of Mt. Jeez.

Again the explanation was simple, as if reality had borne down with a kind of brutal vindictiveness upon one who, in his own world, had often chosen to ignore it. Quite simply, living as he wished to live, never considering illness, my father had spent himself short. His forfeit in the end had been the sale of his forest to pay for the hospital in which he was to die of cancer. He had lent and given often, but he had never borrowed when he was well. To have done such a thing when he knew there was no possibility of his recovery, even though there were many who would gladly have helped him, would have been unthinkable. And so in the end he had had to commit on his own land what he believed to be one of the greatest sins against life, "the ravaging of a forest."

One of those who would have helped in this had she been asked was Doris Duke, who probably knew about his illness better than anyone, and, knowing, had so kindly and quietly offered him refuge while he was being treated. In the same way, after his death, as soon as she knew of the sale of the forest, she bought the timber rights and returned them to my father's estate. So it is thanks to her that gradually the hideous scar has healed over with second growth and the beautiful woods that cover the hills for miles within the view

199

from Mount Jeez have remained intact. I never met Doris Duke, but I know she must have been a profoundly sensitive and good person to have understood and behaved as she did. She must have been aware that, my father being the way he was, there would have been no use in saying, "Let me pay . . . ."

I knew nothing of this then, however. As I looked at the gash in the forest I only knew with a certain deep pride that—in order to remain alone, to be himself—he had had to do what he did. Yet how savage the price and why should it have been so? There is no answer, of course, except that those are the chances of life and each man must take them in his own way. And no one would have been more ready to say so than my father.

I didn't stay long at the farm, for there was nothing there to keep me. Inheritance tax, mortgage and an economic situation that was ruining many a farmer more businesslike than my father had been had made it impossible for us to keep the farm. It had already been sold. I had often hoped that it would fall into the hands of one of those bickering, red-faced farmers who, in their hearts, loved and understood the land as passionately and stubbornly as my father. But beyond this hope, there was nothing I could do.

When I went away, I took with me a sense of futility and unfairness that remained with me for a long time. How unfair it seemed that he should have died alone, ill, not knowing what would happen, probably sure that most of his accomplishments would be destroyed, most likely by the disease of urban spread. It was a certainty I bore, myself, until gradually I came to realize that such energy and zeal for life doesn't so easily disappear. For me it has reappeared and asserted itself at extraordinary moments when indeed, on my part, a great deal of thought has been necessary. Such a moment was when Carson first showed me the land he thought we ought to buy.

I shall never forget my feeling of anticlimax as we stood in the midst of an abandoned plantation of some 80,000 coffee trees, populated by termite and ant hills, its eroded slopes hidden beneath a tangle of junglous second growth and weeds.

"The soil's good," Carson said. And in a gesture I would see repeated countless times during our life together, he bent and dug out a handful of earth with his knife. As he squeezed the clay soil into a ball, rich smelling, moist, and resilient, I had to admit that it was good. Then we walked to the highest point on the land, up against a grove of eucalyptus trees whose branches and gray-green leaves split the light of sunset into long rays across the valley below. It was a broad valley, carved by the meanderings of the ancient River Tieté, which wound its way amid forested and granite strewn hills, pastures of catingueiro grass in purple bloom, croplands of coffee, beans, and rice that was gray-gold and ready for harvest.

"And look, the price is right," Carson went on, as if we'd been talking all the time — which in a way we had, in our minds. For both of us knew that we had just enough money for the first down payment. The rest would have to come from harvesting all the coffee we could get from those poor, neglected trees. From then on it would be a question of putting almost everything we had of money, wit, and work into restoring a pattern of richness and beauty to that abandoned, eroded land. It was an enormous commitment for a family of seven. Yet I really had no trouble in making it. Instead I experienced an airy sense of excitement, rather like what I had felt when we first decided to come to Brazil. And later, an extreme sense of rightness and peace as in the little hotel in the nearby town of Tieté I lay awake thinking about the steps in my life that had, almost without my being aware, guided me to the place where I was.

The knowledge came to me one day in one of those moments in the midst of the half-seeing uncertainty of our lives in which, for some reason, a great many things become suddenly clear.

My family and I had been traveling in Brazil, searching as we still did in our every spare moment for land. After days of driving over the deep-rutted red rivers of roads through an almost uninhabited land of open stretches of wild grasses and dense forests that sloped down, after many miles, to the sea, we came to the edge of a high plateau. Before us, a land broken by steep yellow and ferrous sandstone cliffs slanted down to forests of acacia, cedar, giant peroba and the tall, prehistoric Paraná pine. Behind us, on the plateau, a rich green, fertile land stretched as far as we could see in open fields and knots of shadowy trees. We had no idea to whom the land belonged and only the fact of its great emptiness could have given us the vague hope that it might be for sale. But as we stood looking out from this high place over the lush, green and beautiful land, Carson turned to me suddenly and said, "Well, what do you think?"

Instinctively, without hesitation, as if the words had been sure in my mind for a long time, only waiting for the right moment, I answered, "Yes, of course, this is the right place."

It was, in truth, as awesome and fearful a statement as the taking of a marriage vow, for I knew simply that we meant by this to bind ourselves to this land for life. I knew that I, who loved to be in the center of things, of good company and talk, who loved the theater and had certainly seen only a small part of the world that I wanted to see, would undoubtedly have to forgo a great many of these things, perhaps forever. Yet I also knew, simply and without doubt, that if we devoted ourselves to this land, even if, in the end, we failed, every moment between would be of a rich and real value that none of us would ever regret. It was at this moment as well that with a sudden clarity I understood the reason for this certainty that abolished all the doubt and pessimism I had felt for such a long time.

Those steps had begun when as a child I had stood still on the dunes that edged the forests of Ermenonville to listen to the mating calls of deer, had eaten mushrooms by the firelight in the kitchen and danced in a room strewn with saris in an old Presbytère long ago. It had continued to grow as, later on, I had lived and grown in a house full of music and books, good food and all manner of people from harlots to prima donnas to clergymen and red-faced farmers — all of whom were good people with strong hearts, humor and a tolerant understanding of their fellow men. From that house, I had wandered over the fields of spring, searching among the high grasses for the first shivering lambs. In autumn, I had helped with the harvest and known the special pride and independence of the farmer who, more than any other man, because he lives close to the land, lives close to all that is life. And on many a hot summer day I had followed my father down the middle of Switzer's Creek, halting silently to watch the rise of a crane and then splashing noisily in the cold, cleansing waters of a swimming hole deep in the forest. And quite suddenly, as I thought of this, there came into my mind the words my father had written about Pa in *The Farm* long ago.

"What he gave them was destined to stay with them forever. It was the most precious heritage one could receive. He was a man who knew how to live. He knew the things that count."

And so, quite naturally, with little effort on my part but that of sheer enjoyment, I had come to know the things that counted. It was why I had come as a young girl to live in this distant country, which was, in the beginning, so strange to me, but in which I knew I would find a good life and friends and the exciting knowledge of things I had never before seen. It was why, in the end, I had come upon the rich and fertile and precariously promising land which I knew would one day be mine.

Here, plainly, was my Heritage. And great was my fortune that it had been handed down to me by a lively teacher, a brilliant, temperamental, deeply human man, for whom, just at the mention of a new idea, life had had a way of beginning all over again in all its vigor and beauty, time after time after time.

Postscript

As could well be imagined, the sale of Malabar Farm attracted nearly every variety of the human race. Land speculators would have made of it a "Malabar Village" of split-level houses. Crackpots would have turned it into a retreat for "writers and artists." In the end it was saved from those two unbecoming fates by the Friends of the Land, a group of businessmen and conservationists who, together with the Noble Foundation of Tulsa, Oklahoma, turned it into the Louis Bromfield Ecological Center.

Ecology is the study of man in relation to his surroundings. And, although my father never had much use for the word, it describes in truth the very thing he had done for the last eighteen years of his life.

It was for this in the end that he had made the farm: so that anyone who so desired might walk through the barn, the fields, climb to the top of Mt. Jeez and, in talking with him and looking out over the land, come closer to an understanding of earth and its part in the life of every man.

My father, with the powerful impact of his strong personality, is gone now. But his ideas remain in the memories of those countless people with whom he spoke, and in his writings, all of which are a part of the library at Malabar Farm.

It is to the perpetuation of these ideas that the new Malabar

The Heritage

Farm is dedicated. It is the hope of the Louis Bromfield Ecological Center that those who so desire will come and walk over the land as they did in the past, and, if they feel so inclined, read in the library the things Louis Bromfield would have said to them had he been there to greet them on the lawn.

Epilogue

In his will my father left his estate in trust, to be administered by the law firm of Patterson Belknap and Webb. In doing this, I know that his main concern was our sister Anne who, brilliant and vulnerable, would never be able to live fully on her own. In his heart he must have known that—even without inheritance taxes, mortgage, and an economic situation that was ruining many a farmer— Malabar with its Big House at the center of everything was no guarantee for Annie's needs. Time has proven as well that nothing could have turned out better for everyone concerned than what happened to Malabar Farm as a result.

Today the farm belongs to the state of Ohio. And I am sure no one would be happier than my father that it has become a park with a twist that has made it unique in all the world. For in no other park is there combined an atmosphere in which people may wander amid a wilderness of forests and streams and marshes to come out upon a farm operation, going on in all its integrity. One which, as my father would have had it, considers the orderly farm and the wilderness as parts of an inseparable whole. Nowadays this commonsensical way of looking at things is known as sustainable agriculture and, as when Louis Bromfield was alive, people come by the thousands to ride to the top of Mount Jeez and see what it is all about.

Epilogue

Out of curiosity they come as well to walk through the Big House. To enter, one is obliged to go through a gift shop where once there was a garage, and I will admit that at first this was not an easy thing for me to do. But now I must say I quite enjoy it as I walk through the dining room door to follow enthusiastic guides on what is for me a kind of mystery tour of what was once my home. The more times I go on that tour the more sense it makes to me that everything has been left as it was.

For the French furniture in the living room with its mirrored walls flamboyantly decorated with a golden eagle and stars; the grand piano in the hall where we had held Farmer's Cooperative meetings and danced ballet; the bust of Voltaire in the bay window of my father's bedroom have a particular meaning there that they could never have elsewhere. And as people walk through the house with their dedicated guide reciting Bromfield myths and legends along the way, I'm sure they get a feeling that all the beautiful things within it, gathered from around the world, were a part of every day living. That, rather than collected as an investment, each item once acquired had been placed in a spot someone had in mind for it to occupy, if possible, forever. They belong in an extraordinary house, which is part of a farm where, during Louis Bromfield's life, every-thing produced was made use of—from the fruits and vegetables that filled our larder to the profits that were turned back into the land to make it more fertile than it had been when first he found it.

So it is that, thanks to those who run it, now as ever a great deal goes on at Malabar that appeals to every kind of person, from those who are simply curious to those who seek to learn about the prac-ticalities of sustainable farming. And though I would like to see more happen in this latter direction, my greatest gratitude is that, rather than being sacrificed to urban spread, the place has been kept intact, a beautiful piece of Ohio scenery and history that everyone can richly enjoy.

Still, as the house to me has been absented of its soul, when I return to Malabar it is more than anything to look out over that

country from Mount Jeez. And almost invariably when I do, someone asks, "But wouldn't you sometimes like to return to stay? Don't
you feel a nostalgia for the old days?" To be truthful, I can only
answer, "No." Therefore in the shocked silence that generally follows, I hope that my inquirers listen as I go on to say, "because I
think one of the greatest opportunities we can be given is to able to
do our own thing in our own way."

So it is that my sister Hope and her husband Bob have lived for
years in Montana, their ranch a wildlife preserve where, among
other things in a very busy life, Hope gives haven to critters who
have been stolen from their habitat and maltreated by man. It is as
beautiful and peaceful a place as anyone can imagine. And from it,
through the administration of a fund called the Fanwood Foundation, she dedicates herself to helping conservation organizations
establish themselves and work in various corners of the world,
including Brazil. She loves this work and, by it, follows the premise
also laid before her as a child, that the fullest way to live is by doing
what you like to the best of your ability.

For my part, if I've no real nostalgia for Ohio now, I'm sure it is
because when we came to Brazil, we came to stay. And as immigrants do, we brought what mattered most with us in our minds to
root in a new land. Since then I have often laughed, remembering
myself as a romantic young woman of nineteen, jobless but confident, sitting at the kitchen table in Ohio drawing the design of the
house we would one day build in a country we knew of only by
hearsay. Its most important feature, around which everything else
would fall into place, would be a U-shaped patio large enough to
accommodate an enormous tree. And incredibly enough, that's the
house we built, which we have lived in for nearly forty years and
hope to occupy for the rest of our lives.

The enormous tree is a Pau Brasil, the exploitation of which
provided the Portuguese emperors with a means of luxurious living
five hundred years ago. It is a splendid tree whose tannery bark
children peel and use as boats in the bath tub. From within the

labyrinth of its feathery leaves and yellow, orchid-like flowers we can hear the snap and flutter of hummingbirds and watch the housekeeping of finches who glue their porched nests with spittle and spider webs to the utmost ends of its twigs. Beneath its ever-spreading shade our house stands, rambling and many-windowed. With no architect to guide its building, it is full of mistakes that cannot be repaired. But these defects have been softened by green-ery and the treadings of time so that the house has become a part of everything around it until it no longer matters which is the front door and which is the back.

What matters is that when people step from the sunlit patio into the coolness of its living room full of unmatched furniture, books, paintings, and treasured bits and pieces collected over the years, they say, "What a pleasant house!" And I think, yes, in fact it is. One whose rooms are worn, its fireplace black with use, its doors always open for the comings and goings of dogs and children and absent-minded grownups on half-forgotten missions. One in which the moment my father entered, he would have felt relievedly at home.

Our favorite meal here is Sunday breakfast. For then there is time for everyone to sit at a table heaped with fruits in season — mangos, bananas, acerolas, guavas, and passion fruit side by side with such "exotics" as grapes and plums and pears. On the sideboard fresh orange juice, pots of hot coffee, and milk stand beside platters of very yellow scrambled eggs found amid overgrown fence rows in the nests of incorrigible, country-bred hens who refuse to sit in a coop. To confront this bounty comes a stream of family and friends who heap their plates and push up their chairs wherever they can. Slow to arrive, they are reluctant to leave for fear of not having the last word. While they remain they participate in a contest that is gener-ally more inclined toward noisy wit than any form of serious discus-sion.

At one such breakfast, I remember the subject was inheritance, which so often brings out the worst in human nature, causing brothers to become enemies embroiled in lawsuits that, someone had duly decided, "Left the lawyers rich and the brothers with nothing to be heirs to but air." At length, beginning to feel wearied by the thought of dispersal, I decided to relieve myself of its weight by saying, "That's why the only thing we can safely inherit is ideas." For Maurice Vaneaux, a fine actor given to falling into a part at the slightest suggestion, it was the perfect cue. Rising ceremoniously, blue eyes twinkling beneath bristling brows, with broad gestures, he proceeded to distribute ideas among the family heirs. "Ten ideas for Louis Fergus, twelve for Andreas. Umm, I'm afraid I have only nine ideas for you, Amanda. For Caio, six; Camila, two." Rashly generous at first, by the thirteenth grandchild Lisah, there was nothing for our friend to do but work his features into a look of paupered impotency and declare that he had run out of ideas to dispense. In response to which, small but far from easily dismissed, Lisah let out a scream that sent dogs flying out from under the table and salamanders scurrying up the walls.

How I wished at the time and often have before and afterward that, by some supernatural feat, Louis Bromfield could be with us. Instead, just as we had reached the moment when at last we could talk as adults and friends, our conversations had been brought abruptly to an end. What a good time my father would have had at that breakfast table that reflected so many memories of his own.

Breakfast over, boxer dogs in tow, we would then have walked together out over the fazenda — perhaps to the top pasture to catch sight of a Santa Gertrudis "babá" cow keeping watch over a gang of naughty calves while their mother cows spread out to graze. Or we'd have made our way down to the fields where we plant numerous varieties of bermuda grasses for hay as well as root stock to be used in the forming of pastures everywhere in Brazil. With what pleasure my father would have noted that, in these crop lands once creased by gullies, there was no such thing as erosion. And that as the grass roots formed their protective tangle, they also rotted to create a balance in soils which, scourged by a punishing sun and torrential rains, are always in need of new organic matter. All this we would have discussed in the shade of pecan trees from which whatever nuts are left by marauding parrots and hawks provide a second harvest in what nowadays is known as "layered agriculture."

Talking along the way about legumes and rhizomes and stolons, we'd have walked on to the vegetable garden where at one end a fence is entirely lost in a hedge of blackberry brambles; at the other a tangle of passion fruit vine. Mango and papaya trees shade beds where in their different seasons everything grows, from lima beans, eggplant, cucumbers, and peppers to snap peas, lettuces, tomatoes, and cauliflower. What a good time my father and Carson would have had, turning the compost heap to see how it was rotting, and digging into the newly made seedbeds to count the many earthworms in one small turn of a spade.

No doubt if he could have stayed here long enough — in a guest room very much like The White Room at Malabar do Brasil — Louis Bromfield would have met a lot of people who shared the same interests as he. For what with all the business of cattle and grass, Pau D'Alho has in many ways become a converging point for people who love and work with the land. He would have delighted in the yearly futurity we hold for the sale of bulls and heifers for breeding, in which ranchers everywhere take part, from Belem in the Amazon to Santana do Livramento on the Argentine frontier. It is just Louis Bromfield's kind of fiesta in which sometimes the entertainment is a string quartet, sometimes a ballet; and every sort — from the vaqueiros who care for the cattle to Coroneis who own vast stretches of wilderness — mingle to eat, drink, and dance to drums and guitars and violas on the stone-floored patio beneath the Pau Brasil. But even without a fiesta he would discover that this convergence often happens because, just as it did at Malabar in Ohio, the talk in the fields becomes so intense that people end up being invited to supper and to spend the night.

Then, as seated on the veranda we watch the sunset and go on talking, it also often comes to light that, as a young person, our guest had read the books of Louis Bromfield — an experience which had in some way changed his life.

One such person of course was Carlito Aranha, whose creation years ago was Malabar do Brasil. Another, Paulo de Sa, a young agronomist who has a missionary sense about saving and planting the enormous variety of tropical fruit trees which exist in Brazil before they disappear for want of recognition. And who, having read my father's books and my articles, came to know us and to work with Carson and our sons — farmers all — in the technical details of cultivating grass and trees.

Still another is our friend Nonó Perreira, a grower of soya beans, wheat, and corn who, gathering courage from such books as *Pleasant Valley* and *Malabar Farm,* restored the rundown, eroded lands he had inherited in the state of Paraná. There, combining no-till and rotations of his major crops with legumes and rye, he has devised a system he calls "planting in the straw," which has not only increased his production but reduced his expenses in everything from fertilizers to machinery. Unlike the flamboyant Louis Bromfield, this Brazilian farmer is extremely quiet and unassuming. But having taken up the ideas and tried them, talking in his quiet, convincing way, Nonó Perreira has helped countless farmers not only in Brazil but elsewhere in South America, Africa, and even Europe adapt "planting in the straw" to their own conditions.

Ideas, yes. Despite our laughter at the breakfast table, I do believe nothing better can be passed on to future generations than the worthwhile concepts of those who came before us, to be adapted to the world in which we live. In farming the concepts have to do with conserving our precious soil to deliver it in a better state than we found it, for this above all is the source of our survival. Yet for any of us, such practicalities can only make sense if put into a far greater context.

So it is that every morning when Carson and I walk out over the fazenda, we are reminded — perhaps by the poor color of a field, or a fungus growing on the leeward side of a tree — of the infinite details upon which scientists are constantly at work to help farmers make a living from what is perhaps the most complex profession in existence. But if it is also our good fortune to enjoy just admiring the fungus's bright orange beauty, I think our luck has most of all to do with the manner in which we were raised: I, in that unusual background that was part of but not exactly Ohio; Carson in a close-knit but extremely open-minded Jewish family in Brooklyn, New York.

Louis and Mary Bromfield and the widowed Jenny Geld lived worlds apart and yet they had much in common. The Big House at Malabar and the tiny apartment in Brooklyn were both filled with music and books and were alive with comings and goings. All three loved to sharpen their wits with card games and talk and laughter long into the night. So it is not surprising that when they met, they got on like a house afire. But if their friendship and respect went far beyond an evening's enjoyment, I realize now that this was because, though not particularly disciplined, they lived by a similar set of rules and values they could not have escaped even if they'd tried. And these have come to have an ever deeper and more sensible meaning for me as the years have gone by.

As I go over their list I also see that, far from exclusively ours, the values belong to humanity. And if searched for, they can be found in the Bible and in related precepts that have contributed to enlightenment and the continuity of civilization through all the mess that we greedy, self-deceptive humans daily throw in its way.

"Be curious and listen and give value to everything and everyone around you," Solomon said in countless ways, as also did our parents. Certainly, as their disciples, our habit of curiosity helped us here in the beginning to work in a strange atmosphere with tools we had never used; and to listen, most of all, to the people with whom we worked in the fields, whose everyday comprehension of the things around them gave their observations an extraordinary worth.

"Never take yourself too seriously," for as our forebears saw it, "lack of humor is synonymous with that particular lack of balance which leads to tyranny and tragedy." And surely one has only to look at the battles and dictatorships, crusades and "martyrdoms" described in history to see how right they were.

"There is no quality more valuable than beauty." This lesson, a part of daily life, also seems more clear as life continues on. Nothing more beautiful than a tree whose upper branches provide shelter for myriad life, and whose long-cast shadows in slanting sunlight offer peace to every soul. Unless it be a wildwood on the edge of a well-tilled field. For all these are linked to one another, just as the practical is linked with the aesthetic and spiritual to maintain the whole which surely creation meant there to be.

And if such is true, then it must follow that every profession is a worthy one — from those of house and field, to law and trade and teaching, to that of artists without whose depictions our lives would be dull as those of ants. So lucky is he who can choose a profession for which he has a talent, and use it to contribute to this entire scheme. Whose greatest challenge in our era, it strikes me, might well be that of repair.

As a child I often heard Louis Bromfield say that good farming usually begins only when there is no more frontier land left to exploit. Now, living close to one of the earth's last great frontiers, we can sadly see those words are true as ever, though obviously not only where farming is concerned. Everywhere in the world, looking at the decay of inner cities, the squalor of shanty towns; viewing the countryside as it stretches along highways in monotonous neon-lighted strips of parking lots and malls enjoining us to "buy, buy, buy!" it often seems that some single-minded effort is at work, bent on turning our earth into one vast junk heap, crisscrossed by open sewers under a starless sky.

There are those who insist — especially those who live isolated from reality within the modern fortresses of condominiums — that such plundering and waste is necessary to productivity and prog-

215

ress. "To get things started," they say. But one has only to look at the dreariness and ugliness, the filth and misery this causes — oft reflected in the bored, glazed eyes of youth — to see that this cannot be so. Desecrating land, air, and water, and consequently the lives of people, cannot honestly be called productivity, any more than productivity can be meant to create the debt and waste of a throw-away society. It should provide more people with comfort, health, and ease to make them free to enjoy all life has to offer. But rather than this — out of short-sightedness, greed, and indifference — a growing imbalance has been created which indeed, if CIVILIZATION is to survive, will have to be set right, put on an even keel.

Repair being, as it is, always more difficult to achieve than destruction and suffering, it cannot be an easy job. Yet nowadays how much more we know; how many more tools we have to put to use than did our forebears. This being so, as I sit here before my fine tool of a computer, I cannot help but think of the enormous opportunities which exist, to link all our accumulated knowledge with the wisdom passed down to us by others over centuries, to make of this earth a new frontier. One where the most important goal is not a stuffy, nebulous something called "the bottom line," but to enjoy living fully and usefully. And as we do so, seek that balance which can assure the children whom we have put here a world as it was meant to be — in all its bounty, variety and beauty — worthy of the life they have been given.